500017703129

As one of t

Thomas

For more than 135 years our
guidebooks have unlocked the secrets
of destinations around the world,
sharing with travellers a wealth of
experience and a passion for travel.

**Rely on Thomas Cook as your
elling companion on your next trip
d benefit from our unique heritage.**

WIRR

Thomas Cook **traveller** guides

SCOTTISH
HIGHLANDS
Robin Gauldie

Written and updated by Robin Gauldie
Original photography by Scottish Viewpoint Picture Library

Published by Thomas Cook Publishing
A division of Thomas Cook Tour Operations Limited
Company registration no. 3772199 England
The Thomas Cook Business Park, Unit 9, Coningsby Road,
Peterborough PE3 8SB, United Kingdom
Email: books@thomascook.com, Tel: + 44 (0) 1733 416 477
www.thomascookpublishing.com

Produced by Cambridge Publishing Management Limited
Burr Elm Court, Main Street, Caldecote CB23 7NU
www.cambridgepm.co.uk

ISBN: 978-1-84848-369-9

First edition © 2009 Thomas Cook Publishing
This second edition © 2011
Text © Thomas Cook Publishing
Maps © Thomas Cook Publishing/PCGraphics (UK) Limited
Contains Ordnance Survey data © Crown copyright and database right 2010

Series Editor: Karen Beaulah
Production/DTP: Steven Collins

Printed and bound in Spain by GraphyCems

Cover photography © Colin Paterson

Contents

Introduction

Spectacular scenery and landscapes, all steeped in a history that blends romantic fantasy with bloody and often tragic reality; wide open spaces that make up Britain's only real wilderness; unique wildlife, and terrain that lends itself to a whole array of outdoor activities, from canoeing and mountain biking to sailing, hillwalking and fishing – this is a recipe that makes the Scottish Highlands irresistible.

The Highlands are a place of great variety, from the stark beauty of the Grampian Highlands to the stunning coastline of the far northwest and the dark, brooding waters of Loch Ness.

The ruined clan castles that are dotted over the glens and lochsides of the Highlands are an essential part of the region's romantic appeal. But they are also mementos of a unique Celtic way of life that thrived for more than a thousand years before being wiped out over just a few generations.

The Highlands begin almost on the doorsteps of Scotland's biggest cities, less than 90 minutes' drive from Glasgow, Edinburgh, Dundee or Aberdeen. Few other European countries offer such a swift transition from city streets to the empty hillsides and moorland where wild deer roam and golden eagles soar. The switch from the tidy, cultivated farmlands and 'douce' (quiet, sedate) market towns of Lowland Scotland to the wilder landscapes of the Highlands can be surprisingly sudden.

There is no hard and fast definition of where the Lowlands end and the Highlands really begin, but most people would agree that the unofficial border lies roughly along an imaginary line running diagonally across Scotland from the north shore of the Firth of Clyde to the south shore of the Moray Firth, west of Aberdeen.

There are few cities and only a handful of towns of any size in this part of the world, and even villages are few and far between. Perth, around 80km (50 miles) north of Edinburgh, is the gateway to the Highlands, while Inverness, around 145km (90 miles) further north, is the region's northern hub.

Scotland has a total population of around 5.5 million people, but fewer than 1 million of them live north of the Highland Line.

But this is part of the appeal of the Highlands. South of the Great Glen rise the Grampian Highlands, dominated by some of Scotland's highest peaks and surrounding the magnificently wild Cairngorms National Park. West of these lie the hills and lochs of Perthshire and Argyll, with Ben Nevis looming over the west end of the Great Glen.

North of the Great Glen, the land is even emptier and the vistas even more sweeping. Few places in the world can compare with the beauty of the far northwest coast.

Urquhart Castle beside Loch Ness, near Drumnadrochit

Introduction

The land

The Highlands region is the least populated part of the British Isles, and this – for many visitors – is part of its appeal. Landscapes range from the grandeur of Loch Ness and the Great Glen to smaller, gentler glens, deep sea lochs, and open moorland dotted with tiny, clear tarns, where scarlet dragonflies flit and fierce little brown trout rise to the fisherman's bait. Above all, this is a land of rock and water.

Climate

The tail end of the Gulf Stream takes the chill off the Atlantic coast, which is notably warmer (and wetter) than the North Sea coast. Sub-zero temperatures are common on higher ground, and snow can fall from October onwards and remain until May on the hills, but snow and freezing weather are less common on the coasts and lower ground. Rainfall is high all year round, and summer temperatures rarely rise above 20°C (68°F) – though freak highs of up to 30°C (86°F) have been recorded on rare occasions. This far north, there are long hours of daylight from June to August, with only around four to five hours of darkness at midsummer.

Geology

The advance and retreat of glaciers during several Ice Ages has strongly marked the ancient rocks of the Highland landscape, scouring and smoothing outcrops of red sandstone and grey granite and scattering erratic boulders across glens and moorland. There are likewise outcrops of schist (a metamorphic rock that can be split into thin layers), and veins of semi-precious stones including garnet, tourmaline, amethyst and rose quartz. The Highlands have also given a name to the metallic element strontium, which was discovered in lead mines at Strontian in 1787, and – though not in commercial quantities – gold is found in the River Helmsdale in Caithness.

The Great Glen, a long rift valley that forms a chain of deep, narrow lochs, cuts across the Highlands from the Moray Firth to the Atlantic. At its eastern end, Loch Ness, at 36.4km ($22^2/_3$ miles) long, is the longest body of fresh water in Britain. The Highlands also have Britain's deepest lake, Loch Morar, with a depth of 310m (1,017ft).

Peat beds, formed by ancient deposits of sphagnum moss, are a typical feature of Highland geography. In this mainly treeless region, dried peat has always

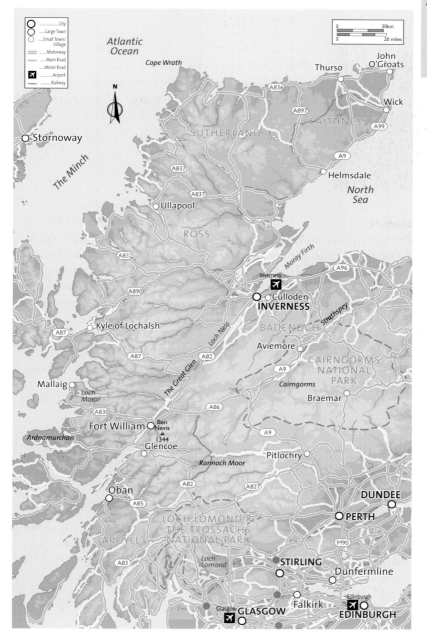

Key:
- ○ City
- ○ Large Town
- ○ Small Town/Village
- ░░░ Motorway
- ─── Main Road
- ─── Minor Road
- ✈ Airport
- ─── Railway

Atlantic Ocean

Cape Wrath

Thurso

John O'Groats

A836

A897

Wick

CAITHNESS

A99

SUTHERLAND

Stornoway

A9

The Minch

A837

Helmsdale

A837

North Sea

Ullapool

ROSS

A832

Moray Firth

A96

A890

Inverness ✈

Culloden

INVERNESS

Kyle of Lochalsh

BADENOCH

Strathspey

A87

A87

Loch Ness

Aviemore

A9

CAIRNGORMS NATIONAL PARK

Mallaig

A82

The Great Glen

Cairngorms

Loch Morar

Braemar

A830

A86

Ardnamurchan

Fort William

Ben Nevis ▲ 1344

A9

Glencoe

Rannoch Moor

Pitlochry

A82

A827

DUNDEE

Oban

A85

PERTH

LOCH LOMOND & THE TROSSACHS NATIONAL PARK

M90

ARGYLL

STIRLING

A83

Loch Lomond

Dunfermline

Glasgow ✈ GLASGOW

Falkirk

Edinburgh ✈ EDINBURGH

been a valuable source of fuel and is still used in some homes. The vast, flat peat bogs of the Caithness Flow Country, on the east coast, make a stark contrast with the hills that dominate the rest of the Highlands.

The hills

Despite their beauty, the Scottish mountains are mere molehills in comparison with the summits of Europe's major mountain chains. Ben Nevis, the highest peak in the UK, is only 1,344m (4,409ft) in height, and only a few other 'bens' (a Gaelic word for mountain peak) top the 1,000m (3,280ft) mark. In fair weather, any of the summits is accessible to any reasonably fit adult. 'Munro-bagging' – attempting to climb all the summits

over 3,000ft (914.4m) in height – is a popular lifetime pursuit.

Lochs and rivers

The rivers and lochs of the Highlands provide Scotland with the key ingredient for one of its major exports, malt whisky, for which a regular, pollution-free supply of pure, fresh water is essential. Scottish waters also lure anglers, and fishing on a legendary salmon river such as the Tay or the Spey costs princely sums in season. Salmon numbers are in worrying decline, and since 2008 anglers on the Tay are permitted to take home only one trophy fish per day, and must release any others that they catch. Brown trout are another catch prized by anglers, and are found in lochs and

Fort William with the substantial mass of Ben Nevis behind

Looking down the length of Loch Ness – all 23 miles of it

rivers. Sea trout inhabit Highland rivers and sea lochs. Britain's rarest fish, the Arctic charr, is found in a few lochs.

The coasts

Northern Scotland is washed by two seas – the Atlantic Ocean to the west, and the North Sea to the east. The west coast is deeply indented by long sea lochs, interspersed by long, sweeping bays and superb sandy beaches. Anywhere else in the world, these would be lined with holiday hotels, but the Scottish climate has spared them the excesses of tourism development. Not far offshore lie the lovely islands of the Inner Hebrides, many of which can easily be visited from the mainland. Skye, the most popular of all, is now reached by a new and controversial road bridge. Forbidding sea cliffs, deep sea caves and tall rock pinnacles known

as stacks are features of the less gentle north coast, which runs between the aptly named Cape Wrath with its swirling breakers in the west, to John O'Groats and the northernmost tip of mainland Britain in the east.

Both Atlantic and North Sea waters shelter a wide variety of marine life, and rock pools at low tide can resemble miniature aquariums, stocked with small rock-dwelling species such as blennies, crabs, shrimp, shellfish, starfish, sea urchins and sea anemones. Herring, haddock and cod, which once formed the basis of a prosperous fishery, have suffered severe decline due to commercial overfishing. The most spectacular inhabitant of Atlantic waters is the enormous basking shark. This intimidating-looking but harmless plankton feeder can be seen in inshore waters off the west coast in summer.

Highland wildlife

Britain's largest mammal, the red deer, flourishes on Highland hillsides and in so-called 'deer forests', which are actually tracts of moorland with hardly a tree in sight. Deer stalking is still a popular (if very exclusive) pastime and is justified on the grounds that herds need to be culled to ensure sufficient grazing for the survivors. The Perthshire and Argyll hills, which are more heavily wooded, are home to roe deer.

Other mammals include badger, pine marten, the increasingly endangered red squirrel, hare, stoat and weasel, and small rodents including the field mouse and harvest mouse. In snowy winters, mountain hare and stoat both adopt white coloration for camouflage. The fur of

A golden eagle, Britain's largest bird of prey

the white stoat, known as ermine, was highly prized in medieval times and still adorns royal ceremonial robes. The magnificent Scottish wildcat is rarely seen and is severely endangered – no longer by hunting but by interbreeding with domestic strays. Otters, though, have recently made a comeback and are not uncommonly seen in rivers and lochs, as well as on the Moray Firth and Atlantic coasts, and beavers, formerly extinct, have been reintroduced to Argyll.

Sea mammals
Offshore, northern waters shelter several spectacular sea-mammal species. The Moray Firth has a thriving bottlenose dolphin population, and porpoise and minke whale may also be seen here.

Off the west coast, migratory minke whale, dolphin and, more rarely, humpback whale and orca are also seen. Seals – grey and common – are easy to spot in western sea lochs.

Birds
The golden eagle, Britain's largest bird of prey, is a potent symbol of the Highlands. Like other raptors, it has suffered greatly at the hands of egg

ANCIENT WILDLIFE

Bear, boar, beaver and wolf were among the large mammals which roamed the Highlands in ancient times. Wolves survived until the 18th century; the last Scottish wolf was killed at Tomalin in 1743. Scotland (like England) probably already has a small breeding population of wild boar, descended from animals that have escaped from boar ranches. Reindeer have also been introduced, and roam semi-wild on some Highland estates.

collectors, gamekeepers and farmers, and from habitat loss, and is listed as endangered. Osprey, red kite and white-headed sea eagle, once extinct, have been successfully reintroduced.

Highland moors are the natural habitat of game birds, including black and red grouse and partridge. The spectacular capercaillie prefers conifer woodland, while the ptarmigan is a denizen of the higher slopes.

Kingfisher and dipper can be seen on rivers and streams, and lochs and sea lochs attract a large number of waders, waterfowl and divers such as merganser and great northern. Greylag, pinkfoot and white-fronted geese are winter migrants.

On sea coasts, eider duck, shag and cormorant are common, and puffin, guillemot, razorbill and gannet roost on cliffs and islets.

Reptiles and amphibians

Harsh winters make the Highlands a hostile habitat for reptiles and amphibians and only a few species are found. These include the common frog and common toad, both of which are most easily seen during their March–April breeding season in ponds and small lochs. Smooth newts and palmate newts are also easiest to see at this time of year, when they gather in numbers to breed in marshy pools. The only reptiles are the common lizard and the adder, both of which have adapted to the short Scottish summer by bringing forth live young. The adder has a venomous but non-lethal bite; it is also extremely shy.

Insects

It sometimes seems that the commonest life form in the Highlands is the dreaded midge, a tiny, bloodsucking fly that appears in swarms in summer and can turn a pleasant day's walking or fishing into a miserable experience. Much more attractive are the numerous butterfly species, including the common blue, small copper, fritillary, skipper and white, and the peacock, red admiral and small tortoiseshell. The migratory painted lady occasionally reaches the southern Highlands. Day-flying moths include the beautiful black and crimson cinnabar moth, whose black-and-orange striped caterpillars are often found feeding on road verges. Small lochs and marshes are perfect dragonfly habitat.

History

7000– 4000 BC	Mesolithic (Middle Stone Age) settlement in Scotland.
4000– 2000 BC	Neolithic (New Stone Age) era.
1600 BC	Climate change drives settlers from higher terrain.
c. 1000 BC	Beginning of Celtic Iron Age culture.
AD 80–84	Romans penetrate into Caledonia, build a line of forts between firths of Clyde and Forth.
122	Romans fall back to line of Hadrian's Wall in northern England.
143–306	Romans build Antonine's Wall between Clyde and Forth. Series of campaigns fail to quell Picts.
367	Scottish and Pictish invasion of northern Britain.
c. 500	Foundation of kingdom of Dal Riada in Argyll by Scots from northern Ireland.
563	Irish missionaries bring Christianity to Scotland.
c. 794	Viking raids begin. Norsemen settle in Orkney, Caithness, Sutherland and Western Isles.
843	Merger of Scots and Pictish kingdoms under the rule of Kenneth MacAlpin, High King of Scots.
c. 889	Donald II of Dal Riada becomes first *Ri Alba* (King of Scotland), reigning until 900.

PICTS AND ROMANS

From around 1000 BC, a Celtic people later known as the Picts (their own name for themselves, along with their language, is lost to history) settled all of Scotland. Standing stones and the stone towers called brochs are the most prominent relics of these Iron Age inhabitants. In AD 82, the Picts resisted a Roman invasion led by the general Agricola. According to the Roman historian Tacitus (Agricola's son-in-law), they were defeated at Mons Graupius, somewhere in the Grampian hills. The Romans made several further efforts to conquer Caledonia (their name for northern Britain) and build a defensive wall from the Firth of Clyde in the west to the Firth of Forth in the east, but made no further inroads into the Highlands.

1296–1328	Scottish wars of independence against England. Highlanders fight for Robert Bruce, King of Scots, at the decisive Battle of Bannockburn, 1314.
1411	Open war in the Highlands between the Crown and Donald, Lord of the Isles, ending with Battle of Harlaw. Both sides claim victory but the Lordship of the Isles remains independent and in control of much of the Highlands.
1428–30	James I again tries to subjugate the Highlands. Alexander, Lord of the Isles, submits but rebels again two years later, defeating a royal army at Inverlochy.
1476	Submission of the Lordship of the Isles and Earldom of Ross to the Crown.
1504–7	Rising of Donald Dubh, Lord of the Isles, quelled by James IV with the help of the powerful Earl of Argyll and the Earl of Huntly.
1508	Earl of Huntly is made hereditary Sheriff of Inverness with a royal remit to pacify the Highlands.
1603	Union of Scottish and English crowns. King James VI of Scotland becomes James I of England.
1604	Proscription of Clan MacGregor.
1637	Rebellion of Scottish 'Covenanters' in Lowlands.
1642	English Civil War begins.
1644–6	Earl of Montrose campaigns in the Highlands for King Charles I but attracts little support from the clans.
1650	Cromwell's conquest of Scotland.
1654	Royalist rising in the Highlands, led by Earl of Glencairn, quickly quelled.
1678	Highland troops used against Lowland Covenanters by the restored royal government of Charles II.
1689	Government forces defeated at Killiecrankie.

1692 Massacre of Glencoe. Campbell soldiers acting on the orders of Sir John Dalrymple of Stair, Scottish Secretary of State, murder 38 men, women and children of the MacDonald clan of Glencoe after their chief delays signing an oath of allegiance to the Crown.

1715–16 First Jacobite Rising, in support of James Stuart (the 'Old Pretender'), ends after defeat at Preston in Lancashire.

1716–36 General Wade, government commander in the Highlands, begins building military roads and forts to pacify the region. Construction of garrison forts at Fort George, Fort William and Fort Augustus along the Great Glen.

1719 Battle of Glenshiel. Destruction of Eilean Donan Castle.

1745–6 Second Jacobite Rising, in favour of Charles Edward Stuart, is initially successful but is finally defeated at Culloden and is followed by massacres of Highland clansmen and civilians by English and Lowland troops.

1751 Publication of the first collection of original verse in Gaelic, *Ais-eiridh na Sean Chanain Albannach* (*The Resurrection of the Old Scottish Language*) by Alasdair Mac Mhaighstir Alasdair.

The remains of Clava Cairns, a group of ancient burial chambers near Culloden

1752	Colin Campbell of Glenure killed in the unsolved 'Appin Murder', which later features in *Kidnapped* by Robert Louis Stevenson.
1776	Publication of the first collection of Gaelic poetry of Mary MacLeod (c. 1615–1707).
1784	Restoration of estates confiscated from Jacobite landowners.
c. 1792–1870	Thousands of crofters (small tenant farmers) driven from their farms by landlords in the 'Highland Clearances' to make way for more profitable sheep farming.
1810	Ben Nevis officially confirmed as Britain's highest peak.
1816	Small Stills Act against illegal whisky-making.
1847–50	Famine in Highlands as potato blight destroys crops.
1886	Crofters' Holdings Act gives them secure tenure and fixed rents.
1891	Sir Hugh Munro publishes first list of 284 Scottish mountains over 3,000ft (914.4m) high.
1894	Completion of West Highland Railway between Fort William and Glasgow.
1940	Capture of the 51st Highland Division in northern France, following the evacuation of Dunkirk.
1974	World's largest oil platform, Highland One, launched at Nigg.
1976	Crofting Reform Act gives crofters the right to buy their land for the first time.
1999	First MSPs elected to new Scottish Parliament.
2006	Smoking banned in all enclosed public spaces.
2007	Scottish National Party breaks Labour's eight-year dominance of Scottish Parliament, pledging to push for full independence.
2011	Highland ports (Campbeltown, Oban and Ullapool) host Tall Ships Race.

The Highland Clearances

The history of the Highlands is the story of a clash of cultures and a long struggle for dominance between Lowlander and Highlander, but Picts and Romans, Scots and English, Vikings and Christian monks, kilted clansmen and Hanoverian redcoats have all left their mark on this dramatic landscape. Highland oral history speaks of 'the great hatred of Gall [Lowlander] for Gael' – a hatred that was rooted in a deep suspicion, among the Scots of the settled Lowlands, towards the unruly Highlanders. The grim drama and romance of that era are still everywhere in evidence, and are part of the unique appeal of this fascinating part of the world.

The Highland way of life – feuding between clans, subsistence farming and fishing supplemented by cattle raiding on the side, with little attention paid to the Crown in Edinburgh or London – persisted for a surprisingly long time, aided by hostile terrain that made quelling the clans difficult.

But the defeat of the Jacobite cause at Culloden spelt the end of the clan era. The Duke of Cumberland's troopers hunted down and murdered those suspected of rebel sympathies. Some of the clan chieftains went into exile in France, but more eventually swore allegiance to the Crown. Military roads and a line of garrison forts were built to enforce government control.

In the century that followed, the Highlands changed more rapidly than ever before. Clan chiefs abandoned their lands and clansmen for the airs and graces of Edinburgh and London. Highlanders were banned from carrying weapons and all the old ways of life, from the pipe to the tartan, were also proscribed – at least for a while.

Memorial cairn at the site of the Battle of Culloden

The difficult terrain in the Highlands gave the clans some protection

By the late 18th century, Highland landowners and Lowland and English investors realised that there was more profit to be had from flocks of sheep than from the rents paid by Highland crofters. Over the next 60 years, thousands of Highlanders were cleared from their lands by force. Some went to live in the new industrial boom city of Glasgow. Others emigrated to Canada and other British colonies, and soon sheep far outnumbered people in the glens. Popular sentiment still blames the English for this, but in fact the clan chiefs were just as keen to evict their tenants.

The evictions began as early as 1814, and over the next decades glen after glen was emptied of its people by truncheon-wielding constables and militia. The people of Ross, Cromarty and Sutherland, and of the islands of the Outer Hebrides, suffered most, for the land that they farmed was poorer and seen by the landowners as more suitable for large flocks of sheep than small herds of the black cattle that Highlanders had always kept. The pace of the evictions speeded up after the potato crop failed due to disease in 1846–7, bringing many people to the edge of starvation and making it easier to persuade them to give up their land and emigrate. By the late 19th century, tens of thousands of Highlanders had emigrated to Canada, to the US, to Australia, South Africa, New Zealand and other British colonies. Few of them ever returned, but Gaelic culture still thrives in unlikely parts of the world such as Nova Scotia.

Politics

Since 1999, Scotland as a whole has been governed by the devolved Scottish Parliament (widely referred to as Holyrood, after its official headquarters in Edinburgh), but has remained part of the United Kingdom. Extensive powers, such as taxation, much legislation and defence, remain under direct control of the UK government in London.

The area covered by this book is divided between four regional authorities: Strathclyde (Argyll), Tayside (Perthshire), Grampian (Grampian Highlands) and Highlands and Islands (everything north of the Great Glen). Strathclyde is administered from Glasgow, Tayside from Dundee (all Lowland cities), Grampian from Aberdeen and Highlands and Islands from Inverness.

Political parties

The regions covered by this book are divided into seven Scottish constituencies, each of which elects a constituency Member of the Scottish Parliament (MSP), along with several regional or 'list' MSPs.

In the 2007 elections to the Scottish Parliament, the Scottish National Party (SNP) won a narrow victory over its chief opponent, Scottish Labour, with 47 seats to Labour's 46. The SNP was strong in the Highlands and northern Scotland, and held five of the seven mainland seats (in Strathclyde, Tayside,

Grampian and the Highlands and Islands), with the remaining two held by the Liberal Democrats, Scotland's third party. The 2010 UK general election saw the Conservative Party triumphant in England but not in Scotland, where they won just one seat. The election underlined the political schism between Highland Scotland and the urban Lowlands: the Liberal Democrats retained the four Highland seats they already held, while the SNP hung on to its one, leaving the Labour Party with no Highland constituencies. Meanwhile, the financial crisis of 2008–9, when the UK government had to rescue the Royal Bank of Scotland, led many people to question whether Scotland could survive economically outside the UK. The SNP's performance in the 2010 UK elections was lacklustre, and independence no longer seems likely in the foreseeable future.

The remoter parts of the Highlands remain strongly dependent on subsidies, job-creation projects and

SCOTS AND SAXONS

After the Romans left Britain, Anglo-Saxons from across the North Sea began to settle in eastern Caledonia, while Scots from Ireland founded the kingdom of Dal Riada in Argyll. Scots kings intermarried with Pictish dynasties, and a culture that fused Anglo-Saxon and Celtic influences began to emerge. By the 8th century, this became the Kingdom of the Scots, known to its people as Alba. By the 10th century, the Celtic languages had been replaced in much of the Lowlands by Scots, a language related to, but distinctly different from, medieval English. The Scots monarchs laid claim to all of Scotland, but the Highlands remained overwhelmingly Gaelic-speaking and Celtic in culture.

incentives for inward investment from the UK government and the European Union. Energy policy is an emotive political issue throughout Scotland. Many Highlanders point out that an independent Scotland could be self-sufficient in energy terms, with an extensive hydroelectricity-generating industry already in place, wind power proliferating across much of the region, and Scottish companies leading the way in the development of new technologies such as wave power.

Landownership is another emotive issue, with a certain amount of resentment of millionaire investors from elsewhere in the UK, mainland Europe and the US who have purchased large Highland estates – among them, the Egyptian millionaire Mohamed Al-Fayed, former owner of the famous Harrods department store, and the pop singer Madonna.

The Scottish Parliament Building in Edinburgh

Culture

Music, poetry and song are at the very heart of the traditional Gaelic culture of the Highlands. Medieval clan chiefs maintained bards whose poetry celebrated their victories and martial prowess and who – in a mainly non-literate society – were also the clans' official historians and genealogists.

Music, verse and dance

Highland culture was mainly non-literate until the 19th century, when the work of such Gaelic bards as Mary MacLeod (c. 1615–1707) began to be published, both in Gaelic and in translation. The banning of many of the trappings of Highland culture, the break-up of the clan system, and the mass emigration of the 19th century, meant that much of the original Gaelic culture was lost, though many songs were preserved by emigrants such as the Nova Scotia-born singer Mary MacDonald (1848–1948).

Highland music and song survived, but sometimes in a popularised form, peddled by kilted crooners such as Harry Lauder and Andy Stewart. The pipe music of the clans mutated into the martial music of the pipe and drum bands of the Highland regiments of the British Army, and also into a vast body of music to which traditional Highland dances – many of them invented as recently as the 19th century – are still performed. Since the 1960s, however, there has been a strong renewal of interest in authentic Gaelic music, song and poetry. The Royal National Mod, first held in 1892 and held every year since then (except during the two world wars) at a different Highland venue, is the greatest celebration of Gaelic music, song and dance; other Mods are held throughout the world (especially in the US, Canada and Australia) wherever the descendants of Highland emigrants are found. The ceilidh – an evening of music, dancing and drinking – is no less of a Highland institution, held in all sorts of town and village venues, and is a less formal celebration of Highland culture, often blended with more modern musical contributions from bands such as Runrig, whose music fuses traditional influences with rock.

Literature and theatre

In contrast to its rich oral and musical tradition, Highland literature has a less impressive record. *Kidnapped*, the best

Highland adventure yarn ever written, was the work of a Lowland Scot, the Edinburgh-born Robert Louis Stevenson. Sir Walter Scott, author of *Rob Roy*, was another Lowlander who drew inspiration from the romance of the Highlands, as was John Buchan, author of *The Thirty-Nine Steps*, who set several of his tales among the glens and moors. *The Cheviot, the Stag and the Black, Black Oil*, written by John McGrath and designed for the stage by Scots playwright John Byrne, deals with the changes wrought on Highland and Scottish culture over two centuries by the advent of huge sheep flocks, private deer reserves and most of all by the impact of the oil industry. Caithness author Neil M Gunn drew inspiration from the Highlands for many of his books, including works such as *Butcher's Broom*, his story of the Clearances.

Hamish Henderson, one of Scotland's greatest 20th-century poets, balanced Highland and Lowland influences in much of his work. The multi-talented Gavin Maxwell, author of *Ring of Bright Water*, painted and wrote about his life with Highland sea otters at Sandaig, near Glenelg on the west coast, in stories that captured the imagination of the public.

Visual arts
The ancient Celtic and Norse cultures of the Highlands and Isles during the Dark Ages and early medieval times produced a strikingly rich trove of visual arts, notably highly decorated

A Highland dancing competition in Argyll

Glen Nevis: provided a backdrop for Scotland's heroes and villains

gold and silver jewellery and carved wood and stone in the distinctive and intertwined pattern known as knotwork.

The Highlands have produced no towering visual talents in modern times, but their scenery inspired a generation of 19th-century landscape painters such as the Glaswegian Horatio McCullough (1805–67), whose gloomily romantic paintings of glens and waterfalls pandered to the Victorian image of the Highlands, while Sir Edwin Landseer's *Monarch of the Glen*, painted in 1851, with its image of a noble stag, is probably the best-known painted image of the Highlands in the world. Contemporary painters include Ullapool-based James Hawkins, who produces dynamic, colourful versions of Highland landscapes and seascapes.

Cinema and television

The landscapes that inspired Victorian painters have also provided the setting for an impressive array of films. *Rob Roy* (1995), starring Liam Neeson, and *Braveheart* (1995), starring Mel Gibson, were both shot partly in Glen Nevis, in the shadow of Scotland's highest mountain. *Local Hero* (1983), directed by Bill Forsyth and starring Burt Lancaster, is set in a fictional west coast village, though it was in fact shot on the Aberdeenshire coast. *Highlander* (1986) is an entertaining piece of hokum, with French actor Christopher Lambert playing the clansman who becomes an immortal warrior with an accent that is more Gallic than Gaelic, and a cameo role for Scots actor Sir Sean Connery. *Mrs Brown* (1997), set on Deeside, stars Dame Judi Dench as the widowed Queen Victoria and Billy Connolly as her favourite Highland ghillie, John Brown. Rannoch Moor provides the setting for a scene from *Trainspotting* (1996), notable for a superb rant by its anti-hero Renton (Ewan McGregor) on Scotland's pusillanimous relationship with England and with its own culture. *Trainspotting* also featured Robert Carlyle, who went on to play the eponymous Highland village policeman in the TV series *Hamish Macbeth* – filmed in and around Plockton – and other soaps set in the Highlands have included *Take the High Road*, shot in and around Luss, on Loch Lomond, and the BBC series *Monarch of the Glen*, set in fictional Glenbogle and filmed at Ardverikie House, on Loch Laggan, which was also a location for *Mrs Brown*.

Folklore and legends

Christianity arrived in the Highlands by the 6th century, but although the Highlands paid lip service to the early Celtic Church, then to the Roman Church, many pre-Christian beliefs and superstitions seem to have survived. The Picts and other Celts venerated a pantheon of water deities, and these have survived as legends of an array of mischievous and sometimes murderous water spirits. The river-dwelling kelpie was said to sometimes lure travellers into treacherously deep pools or bogs. The *each uisge* (water horse), which lived in lochs or sea lochs, took the form of a beautiful steed, then carried anyone foolish enough to mount it into the depths, there to be devoured. The selkie – which could change its form from seal to human – was less malicious. Legends of the Sidhe (pronounced 'Shee') – a beautiful, powerful, immortal fairy race – lived on into modern times and are reflected in place names like Glen Shee and Schiehallion, whose name means 'holy place of the Sidhe'. Other long-standing Highland superstitions are belief in the 'second sight' – an ability to see into the future. White flowers are associated with death, and it is considered unlucky to bring them into any home.

Part of the film *Highlander* was set in Eilean Donan Castle

Festivals and events

Venues around the Scottish Highlands host an exciting variety of cultural, musical and sporting events throughout the summer, ranging from open-air rock and pop gigs to traditional music and poetry festivals, as well as the tartan pageantry of several dozen Highland Games, where kilted strongmen, pipe bands and traditional dancers show off their skills. The busiest time of year is from May to September, but there are also local events in the Christmas season, culminating in the national New Year celebration.

February
Fort William Mountain Festival
One-week celebration of mountain culture and adventure, with films, talks by mountaineering legends, mountain-skills workshops, a photo competition and other events.
The Highland Mountain Culture Association, PO Box 7035, Fort William PH33 6WR. Tel: (01397) 700 005. www.mountainfestival.co.uk. Admission charge.

June
RockNess
Scotland's coolest rock and dance music festival, with bands and top DJs, lasts through a weekend in June, at Dores, just outside Inverness on the banks of the loch.
Dores Road, Dores. No tel. www.rockness.co.uk, tickets from www.ticketline.co.uk and www.tickets-scotland.com. Admission charge.

July
Tulloch Inverness Highland Games
Throwing the hammer and tossing the caber are some of the highlights of one of the biggest events in the Highlands, along with dancing, pipe bands and a clan gathering.
Bught Park, Inverness. Tel: (01463) 663 823. www.invernesshighlandgames.com. Organisers: Inverness Highland Games Committee, The Highland Council, The Town House, Inverness IV1 1JJ. Admission charge.

August
Nairn Jazz Festival
This festival makes a welcome change from the sound of the pipes, attracting world-class jazz artists in early August.
136 High Street, Forres IV36 1NP. Tel: (01309) 674 221. www.nairnjazz.com. Admission charge.
Belladrum Festival
The top alternative festival in the Highlands, with music ranging from

traditional ceilidh foot-tappers to reggae, rock and avant-garde.
Belladrum Estate, Beauly IV4 7BA.
Tel: (01463) 741 336.
www.tartanheartfestival.co.uk.
Admission charge.

Inverness Book Festival
This popular literary event brings young and adult readers and authors together for readings, family events and workshops for budding writers.
Eden Court Theatre, Inverness.
Tel: (01463) 234 234.
www.invernessbookfestival.co.uk.
Admission charge for some events –
see website.

September
Royal Braemar Gathering
Patronised by the Royal Family since Queen Victoria's time, this is the grandest of the Highland gatherings and is held on the first Saturday in September. The day's schedule includes competitions for dancing, piping, caber-toss, stone-putting, tug-of-war and so on.
Braemar Royal Highland Society,
Braemar AB35 5YG.
Tel: (01339) 741 098.
www.braemargathering.org.
Admission charge.

Blas
Exciting Gaelic and traditional music festival, with performances by local, national and international artists.
Various venues. Tel: (01463) 225 559.
www.blas-festival.com.
Admission charge.

Loopallu
This family-friendly festival takes place in the third week in September and features everything from rock to pipe bands, street and fringe performances.
Various venues, Ullapool.
Tel: (0871) 230 2360.
www.loopallu.co.uk. Admission charge.

October
**An Mod Naiseanta Rioghail
(Royal National Mod)**
Scotland's premier Gaelic festival, with competitions in music and song, Highland dancing, drama, poetry, sport and literature.
Organisers: 109 Church Street,
Inverness IV1 1EY. Tel: (01463) 709 705.
www.the-mod.co.uk.
Admission charge.

November
St Andrew's Day (30 November)
Scotland's official National Day – minor events nationwide.

December
**Hogmanay
(New Year's Eve, 31 December)**
Scotland's biggest night out is lower key in the Highlands. Inverness has a Hogmanay fireworks display each year. For up-to-date information on other events in the Highlands, *see www.hogmanay.net*
Inverness Castle (best viewed from Ardross Terrace, on the opposite side of the river). 5.30–6pm.
Free admission.

Festivals and events

Highlights

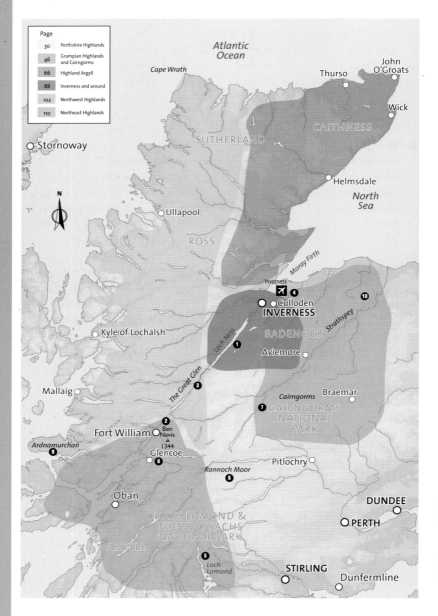

Page	
30	Perthshire Highlands
46	Grampian Highlands and Cairngorms
66	Highland Argyll
88	Inverness and around
102	Northwest Highlands
110	Northeast Highlands

Atlantic Ocean

Cape Wrath

Thurso

John O'Groats

Wick

CAITHNESS

Stornoway

SUTHERLAND

Helmsdale

North Sea

N

Ullapool

ROSS

Moray Firth

Inverness ✈ 4

Culloden
INVERNESS

Kyle of Lochalsh

Loch Ness

1

BADENOCH

Strathspey

10

Aviemore

The Great Glen

3

Mallaig

Cairngorms

Braemar

7

CAIRNGORMS NATIONAL PARK

2
Ben Nevis

Fort William

1344

Ardnamurchan

9

Glencoe

8

Pitlochry

Rannoch Moor

6

Oban

DUNDEE

LOCH LOMOND & THE TROSSACHS NATIONAL PARK

PERTH

ARGYLL

5

Loch Lomond

STIRLING

Dunfermline

Highlights

❶ **Loch Ness** A few miles southwest of Inverness, Loch Ness is 36.4km (22²/₃ miles) in length and up to 213m (700ft) deep, and it is easy to believe that unknown monsters lurk there. The loch is overlooked by one of the most picturesque of Scotland's ruined castles, Urquhart Castle (*see p97*).

❷ **Ben Nevis** Britain's highest mountain is 1,344m (4,409ft) above sea level, but the summit can be reached by any reasonably fit walker. The best views of the mountain are from the Gairlochy road, northwest of Fort William (*see pp66–7*).

❸ **The Great Glen and Caledonian Canal** A remarkable feat of engineering, the Caledonian Canal links Fort William with Inverness by way of the lochs of the Great Glen. The Great Glen makes a spectacular drive, but you can also journey along the canal aboard a rented cruiser (*see pp98–9*).

❹ **Culloden Battlefield** The bleak expanse of Drumossie Moor is where the Highland clans made their last stand against the Duke of Cumberland's redcoats on 16 April 1746 (*see pp88–90*).

❺ **Loch Lomond** Dotted with islands, bordered by a beautiful national park, overlooked by the 973.5m (3,194ft) peak of Ben Lomond, Loch Lomond is a romantic gateway to the Argyll Highlands (*see p77 & pp80–81*).

❻ **Rannoch Moor** The unique 'pocket wilderness' of Rannoch Moor, with its rolling moorland and dozens of small lochs and clear streams, is superb walking territory (*see pp42–3*).

❼ **The Cairngorms** These mountains offer winter sports and a choice of outdoor activities. The Cairngorms National Park provides a refuge for many rare and endangered species (*see pp52–3*).

❽ **Glencoe** Glencoe is one of Scotland's most spectacular glens, and the scene of one of the best-known tragedies in Highlands history – the massacre of the MacDonalds of Glencoe by Campbell soldiers in the service of King William in 1692 (*see pp69–71*).

❾ **Ardnamurchan** This remote peninsula is a beautiful stretch of the northwest coast, with splendid views to the island of Coll, the Sound of Mull and the Sound of Arisaig (*see p102*).

❿ **Speyside Distillery Trail** The banks of the River Spey are home to some of Scotland's best-known single malt whisky distilleries (*see pp59–63 & pp64–5*).

Suggested itineraries

Long weekend: around Inverness

For a three-night break and a sample of the best of the Highlands, start in Inverness. Inverness is accessible by air, train and bus. A car is not essential for this itinerary as all the recommended sights are accessible from Inverness by public transport or as part of a guided tour, which can easily be booked through the tourist office or your hotel (*see p91*).

Day one: visit Fort George and the Highlanders Regimental Museum, the Culloden Battlefield Visitor Centre and the Clava Cairns.

Day two: take a Loch Ness cruise and visit Urquhart Castle and Drumnadrochit to find out about the legendary monster and the ongoing quest for evidence of its existence.

Day three: go on a Moray Firth dolphin-watching cruise from Inverness or take a tour of the Strathspey malt whisky distilleries.

One week: Loch Lomond to Inverness

This itinerary requires a car and covers a distance of around 400km (250 miles).

Day one: fly or drive to Glasgow, then follow the A82 north to Loch Lomond, the romantic gateway to the Argyll Highlands.

Day two: explore the surroundings of the loch, including the Loch Lomond and the Trossachs National Park on the east shore and the pretty lochside village of Luss before driving to Inveraray, on Loch Fyne, taking a break at the famous and appropriately named Rest and be Thankful viewpoint.

Day three: after visiting Inveraray Castle, seat of the dukes of Argyll, drive from Inveraray down the spectacular north shore of Loch Fyne to Lochgilphead, then turn north along the Crinan Canal to the cheery fishing village and holiday resort of Oban, near the mouth of Loch Linnhe.

Day four: drive from Oban to Fort William by way of the Pass of Glencoe (following the A85 to Tyndrum, then the A82 through Glencoe to Fort William). This is a super scenic drive, with views of the 343.2m (1,126ft) Ben Cruachan, the steep slopes of Glencoe and, as you approach Fort William, Britain's highest mountain, Ben Nevis.

Day five: walk to the top of Ben Nevis (*see pp66–7*) or take a seal-spotting cruise from Fort William.

Day six: drive along the Great Glen, the Caledonian Canal and the banks of Loch Linnhe, Loch Lochy and Loch Ness to Inverness.

Day seven: visit Culloden Battlefield and take a Loch Ness cruise or a Moray Firth dolphin- and whale-spotting cruise before returning southwards on the A9 via Perth.

Two weeks: Perth to John O'Groats and back

If you are travelling to the Highlands with your own car, Perth is the most convenient gateway. Alternatively, travel to Perth by train and rent a car. This itinerary covers around 800km (500 miles).

Day one: drive from Perth to Aviemore, stopping en route to visit Blair Atholl and Blair Castle.

Day two: drive from Aviemore through Strathspey to Nairn on the Moray Firth, pausing to visit some of the Speyside distilleries on the way.

Day three: drive from Nairn to Inverness, stopping on the way at Culloden Battlefield and Clava Cairns.

Day four: cruise Loch Ness, then drive to Helmsdale.

Day five: drive to John O'Groats and Duncansby Head, visit the Castle of Mey then drive to Thurso.

Day six: drive to Cape Wrath, then to Scourie and Lochinver.

Day seven: drive to Ullapool.

Day eight: drive from Ullapool to Fort William via Glen Carron and Glen Shiel.

Day nine: climb Ben Nevis.

Day ten: drive from Fort William to Oban.

Day 11: day trip to Isle of Mull from Oban.

Day 12: drive from Oban to Inveraray by way of Lochgilphead.

Day 13: drive from Inveraray to Loch Lomond.

Day 14: visit Loch Lomond and the Trossachs National Park.

Suggested itineraries

The old drovers' road in Glencoe

The Perthshire Highlands

Perthshire, Scotland's largest county, stands between the Highlands and the Lowlands and embraces a remarkable array of scenery, from the fertile farmlands south and east of Perth to the sweeping vistas of Rannoch Moor and Schiehallion, the lochs and salmon rivers of the Tay and Earn valleys and the ski slopes of Glenshee. Its glens are more heavily wooded than most, earning it the nickname the 'Big Tree Country'.

Aberfeldy

Aberfeldy is a pretty, small town set among wooded scenery on the banks of the River Tay, not far from Loch Tay, through which the river flows. It has become a popular centre for all kinds of outdoor activities and adrenalin sports, including canyoning, river rafting, abseiling, kayaking and canoeing. The river provided a reliable source of pure water for one of Aberfeldy's main traditional industries, whisky distilling, and whisky is still made here. Aberfeldy is a good base for exploring Loch Tay, Glen Lyon and the surrounding countryside, and a pleasant overnight stop for those travelling onward to Inverness or west into Argyll.

Castle Menzies

Surrounded by farmland, this small stronghold dates from the 16th century. It was, and still is, the seat of the Menzies (pronounced 'Mingus') clan, has been lovingly restored with money raised by clan members worldwide, and

now houses an eclectic array of Menzies memorabilia. It is a low-key collection, but the castle's small scale is part of its attraction, making it less overwhelming than some bigger and more lavishly furnished stately homes. Charles Edward Stuart is said to have spent a night here on his way to his final defeat at Culloden in 1746.

Weem village, 1km (²/₃ mile) west of Aberfeldy. Tel: (01887) 820 982. www.menzies.org. Open: Apr–Oct Mon–Sat 10.30am–5pm, Sun 2–5pm. closed: Nov–Mar. Admission charge.

Dewar's World of Whisky

This is a traditional working distillery operated by one of Scotland's best-known whisky brands. Interactive visitor centre, tasting sessions and shop.

Aberfeldy Distillery. www.dewarswow.com. Open: Apr–Oct Mon–Sat 10am–6pm, Sun noon–4pm; Nov–Mar Mon–Sat 10am–4pm. Closed: Christmas & 1 Jan.

St Mary's Church
The unassuming exterior of this little 16th-century church conceals a beautiful interior with an outstanding painted ceiling adorned with heraldic symbols.
Pitcairn Farm, Grandtully, 3km (2 miles) east of Aberfeldy centre on the A827. No tel. www.historic-scotland.gov.uk. Open: Apr–Sept daily 9.30am–6.30pm. Closed: Oct–Mar. Admission charge.

Wade's Bridge
Built in 1733 and designed by William Adam, this bridge across the Tay is the most graceful of all the bridges constructed as part of General Wade's network of military roads into the Highlands. Next to it stands the Black Watch Monument, commemorating the officers and men of Perthshire's most famous regiment.
Tay Bridge Drive, Aberfeldy.

Blair Atholl
Blair Atholl, just off the main A9 Perth–Inverness highway, is a small village with just a handful of shops and pubs.
56km (35 miles) north of Perth.

Atholl Country Life Museum
This is a lively, quirky small museum that tells children and adults about life in the Perthshire countryside in bygone times. Exhibits include a smithy, stable, cattle byre and typical cottage living room, old post office and village shop.

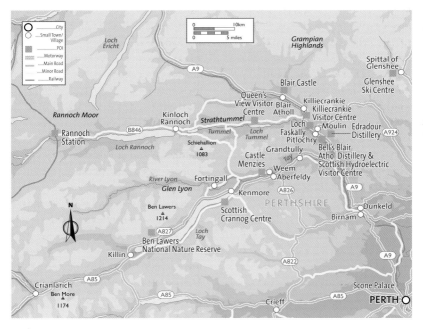

Blair Atholl. Tel: (01796) 481 232. Open: Easter, end May–Jun & Sept daily 1.30–5pm; Jul–Aug daily 10am–5pm. Closed: Easter–end May & Oct–Easter. Admission charge.

Blair Castle

Blair Castle has been the seat of the earls and dukes of Atholl and the Clan Murray for almost 750 years. With its whitewashed stone walls and pointed grey turrets, it is one of Scotland's most enchanting (and most visited) castles. Within is an array of baronial splendour including arms and armour, tapestries, porcelain and silverware, displayed in more than 30 grand salons. On a summer's day, the grounds, with their resident peacocks and ponies, are the perfect place for a stroll or a picnic, and the surrounding scenery is breathtaking. Highland pony trekking, from one hour to a full day's trekking, is also available. Blair Castle is also the home of the Atholl Highlanders, the ceremonial guard of the Duke of Atholl. The right to maintain this private army – the last such force in Europe – is an ancient privilege, dating back to medieval times, when the earls of Atholl ruled this part of the Highlands almost as independent monarchs. Remarkably, this privilege survived the 1745 rising and Culloden, at which Atholl fought with the defeated Jacobites.

10km (6 miles) north of Pitlochry. Tel: (01796) 481 207. www.blair-castle.co.uk. Open: Apr–Oct daily 9.30am–4.30pm. Closed: Nov–Mar. Admission charge.

Looking over the trees towards 13th-century Blair Castle

Dunkeld

Standing on the east bank of the River Tay, which is crossed here by a graceful seven-arched bridge designed in 1809 by the great 19th-century engineer Thomas Telford, Dunkeld is an attractive small town of grey-stone buildings, overlooked by the spire of its attractive cathedral. It's hard to believe now that this peaceful small market town was once the religious capital of Scotland, and thus one of the most important places in the kingdom. Kenneth MacAlpin brought holy relics of St Columba to the monastery of Dunkeld when he moved his capital to Scone in AD 843. It was here in 1689, after the defeat of government troops at Killiecrankie, that the Jacobite Highlanders were stopped in their tracks by a garrison of determined musketeers from the tough Protestant sect known as the Cameronians, after their fiery leader, the preacher Richard Cameron. Dunkeld was heavily damaged during the fighting, and was rebuilt during the 18th century as one of the most gracious small towns in northern Scotland, with broad streets and well-proportioned buildings. On the opposite bank of the Tay, the village of Birnam has now become little more than a suburb of Dunkeld.

Beatrix Potter Garden

Beatrix Potter, author of *The Tale of Peter Rabbit*, *The Tale of the Flopsy Bunnies*, and an array of much-loved children's tales of anthropomorphic bunny rabbits, ducks, frogs, squirrels, hedgehogs and other woodland creatures, holidayed in Birnam as a child and was inspired by its wildlife. Her memorial is the Beatrix Potter Garden, close to the banks of the Tay, with children's activities, performances, a shop, and pottery figures of some of her creations.

The Birnam Institute, Station Road, Birnam, by Dunkeld. Tel: (01350) 727 674. www.birnamarts.com. Open: daily 10am–5pm. Admission charge.

Dunkeld Cathedral

Dunkeld Cathedral stands on the site of a 6th-century chapel and is perhaps the most impressive Christian ruin in the region. Its long nave, dating from the 15th century, has lain roofless since it was sacked by Protestant reformers in 1560, but the choir is still in use as Dunkeld's parish church. Columba's relics, it is claimed, are buried beneath the chancel steps.

Market Square, Dunkeld. Tel: (01350) 727 601. Open: Apr–Sept daily 9.30am–6.30pm; Oct–Mar daily 9.30am–4pm. Free admission.

Fortingall

Built during the 19th century, Fortingall – like Luss, on Loch Lomond (*see p81*) – is a trim and tidy 'model village' laid out by a modernising landowner. But it has ancient roots – literally. In its churchyard stands a huge yew tree that is believed to be as much as 3,000 years old, making it the oldest

The village of Kenmore

Tumbling through the glen, the River Lyon carves its way through rocky passes and boulder-strewn pools and is a noted trout stream. The longest enclosed glen in Scotland, it is 55km (34 miles) in length. The wild, inaccessible country west of Glen Lyon made it a haven for the outlawed MacGregors, and for centuries these hills were contested between the Campbell and MacGregor clans. It was a troop of Campbells of Glenlyon, acting on government orders, who carried out the infamous 'Massacre of Glencoe' in 1692. To this day, there is no road west from the top of the glen.

Loch Tay

Loch Tay is one of Scotland's prettiest lochs. At 23km (14 miles) in length, it is the largest loch in Perthshire, and Perthshire's longest river, the Tay, runs through it. It is overlooked by Perthshire's highest mountain, Ben Lawers. Surrounded by striking mountain scenery, its banks have been inhabited for more than 3,000 years and ancient dwellings have been discovered beneath its waters. It is a popular location for fishing and watersports. **Kenmore**, on the east edge of the loch, has been declared a conservation village and is one of the prettiest villages in Perthshire.

Ben Lawers National Nature Reserve

This nature reserve is on the slopes of Ben Lawers. Perthshire's highest mountain at 1,214m (3,983ft), Ben

life form in Europe. Just outside the village are the scant remains of a Roman camp. This is probably as far north as the Romans ever came. Fortingall is claimed to be the birthplace of Pontius Pilate, who, according to legend, was the son of a Roman father serving with the legions and a Pictish mother, but whether or not this legend has any basis in fact is not known.

Glen Lyon

Heading west from Fortingall into Glen Lyon there is a real sense of passing from civilisation into wilderness – and taking a step back into history. Once populous, Glen Lyon is now almost deserted, and a little eerie, with the toppled stone walls of ancient cottages dotted around its steep slopes.

Lawers overlooks Loch Tay and is renowned for its unique mountain flora. *10km (6 miles) northeast of Killin, off the A827. Nature reserve open: all year daily 24 hours. (The visitor centre has been closed.)*

Scottish Crannog Centre

This excellent re-creation of one of the Iron Age dwellings known as 'crannogs' – thatched houses set above the water on wooden pilings – fascinates visitors of all ages. The reconstruction is based on the remnants of ancient crannogs that have been found beneath the waters of Loch Tay.
1km (²/₃ mile) southwest of Kenmore. Tel: (01887) 830 583. www.crannog.co.uk. Open: Apr–Oct daily 10am–5.30pm; Nov Sat–Sun 10am–4pm. Closed: Dec–Mar. Admission charge.

Perth

During the Middle Ages, the county town of Perth was one of the most important towns in Scotland, and nearby Scone was the earliest capital of the Scottish kingdom. Strategically located at what was the lowest crossing (and highest navigable point) of the River Tay, Perth also stands between the Lowlands and the Highlands, and even after the Scottish capital moved south – first to Dunfermline, then to Edinburgh – Scots monarchs came to Scone to be crowned on the 'Stone of Destiny'.

A view over the calm waters of Loch Tay

Perth today claims to be the gateway to the Highlands and is a prosperous market town on the west bank of the Tay, with good shopping, plenty of places to eat and drink, and a handful of sights worth visiting on your way north. It has a famous race track which draws some of horse racing's most famous names, and is the home of Scotland's oldest kilted regiment, the Black Watch, which is now a battalion (the 3rd) of the Royal Regiment of Scotland.

Black Watch Regimental Museum

Housed in a 19th-century Scottish baronial building, the museum traces the history of the Black Watch, also known as the 42nd Regiment of Foot, from its foundation in 1739 until the present day, with weapons, uniforms, regimental trophies and portraits laid out chronologically in seven rooms. There is also a shop that sells Black Watch official memorabilia, including bonnets, kilts, many a *sgian dubh* (black knife) and copies of the regiment's official dress.

Balhousie Castle, Hay Street.
Tel: (01313) 108 530.
www.theblackwatch.co.uk. Open:
Mon–Sat 9.30am–5pm, Sun (Apr–Oct)
10am–5.30pm. Closed: festive periods –
see website. Admission charge.

Branklyn Gardens

This little garden on the outskirts of Perth, on the opposite bank of the Tay, covers just 0.8 hectares (2 acres) and is now run by the National Trust for Scotland. It is noted for its fine collection of rare and unusual shrubs and flowers, including colourful

Across the River Tay to Perth

rhododendrons, vivid acers and bright blue Himalayan poppies.

116 Dundee Road, 1.5km (1 mile) west of town centre. Tel: (0844) 493 2193. www.nts.org.uk. Open: 31 Mar–31 Oct daily 10am–5pm. Closed: 1 Nov–30 Mar. Admission charge.

Fergusson Gallery

This remarkable gallery – housed in a converted 19th-century waterworks – contains a superb and colourful collection of paintings, drawings and sculpture by one of Scotland's most important painters, John Fergusson (1874–1961), and is one of only four Scottish museums or galleries to be dedicated to the work of a single artist.

Marshall Place. Tel: (01738) 441 944. www.scottishmuseums.org.uk. Open: Mon–Sat 10am–5pm, Sun (May–Sept) 1–4.30pm. Closed: 25 Dec & New Year. Free admission.

St John's Kirk

There has been a church on this site since 1126, but the oldest part of the present-day St John's Kirk is the choir, which dates from the 15th century. The church is Perth's oldest building, and its grey spire is a prominent landmark in the centre of town. The beautiful stained-glass windows, added in 1923–6, are the work of Douglas Strachan, and portray the Last Supper, the Crucifixion, and St John the Baptist, the town's patron saint. The rabble-rousing Protestant reformer John Knox preached here in 1559,

inciting the townspeople to sack Perth's great abbey and other religious foundations. The kirk now belongs to the Church of Scotland, but worshippers of all faiths are welcome.

St John's Square. No tel. www.st-johns-kirk.co.uk. Open: May–Sept Mon–Sat 10am–4pm. Closed: Oct–Apr. Services: Sun 9.30am & 11am. Admission free but donation welcomed.

Scone Palace

Set in manicured grounds overlooking the River Tay, just outside Perth, Scone Palace is one of Scotland's grandest stately homes, with a superb collection of paintings, statuary, silverware, porcelain and antiques amassed over generations by its owners, the earls of Mansfield. Queen Victoria was a guest, and the lavish Queen Victoria Bedroom is one of the palace's highlights. The famous **Stone of Destiny**, on which Scottish monarchs were crowned, is no longer on-site – it was stolen by the English during Edward I's invasion of Scotland during the 13th century, and is now kept in Edinburgh – but there is a replica atop the Moot Hill, in the palace grounds. Farm animals and a flock of peacocks roam in the grounds around the palace, and there is a topiary maze that is excellent for keeping children amused.

Scone, 4km (2½ miles) north of Perth. Tel: (01738) 552 300. www.scone-palace.co.uk. Open: Apr–Oct daily 9.30am–5pm (grounds until 5.45pm). Closed: Nov–Mar. Admission charge.

Walk: Around the fair city (Perth)

This walk through Perthshire's compact and pedestrian-friendly county town starts in the old town centre and visits a working watermill, a regimental museum, two historic churches and an outstanding collection of paintings, ending on the banks of the silvery River Tay.

Allow 3 hours, including visits to museums, galleries and churches.

Start at Lower City Mills, on the corner of the High Street and North Methven Street. The mill building also houses Perth's Tourist Information Centre.

1 Lower City Mills

Water power was one of the sources of Perth's prosperity until the 19th century, and this working mill with its huge waterwheel dates from the Victorian era.

Walk up North Methven Street to the corner of Atholl Street and St Ninian's Cathedral, on your left.

2 St Ninian's Cathedral

This city-centre landmark was built in 1849 and consecrated in 1850, and was the first cathedral to be built in Britain since the Protestant Reformation of the 16th century.

Cross Atholl Street to Melville Street and continue northwest to the corner of Hay Street. Turn right on to Hay Street, then follow the road up to Balhousie Castle.

3 Balhousie Castle and the Black Watch Regimental Museum

This museum is dedicated to Perth's regiment, the Black Watch, and contains a collection of uniforms, portraits, regimental honours, maps and records tracing their campaigns.

Return to the town centre through North Inch Park, Perth's attractive riverside green space. Leave the park at the Rose Terrace gate, turn left and, after crossing Charlotte Street, turn right, then almost immediately left into Kinnoull Street and left again on Curfew Row.

4 The Fair Maid's House

On Curfew Row, this old building with its grey-stone walls and fanciful miniature turret is the oldest house in Perth. Local legend claims it as the home of Catherine Glover, heroine of Sir Walter Scott's medieval romance *The Fair Maid of Perth*.

Follow Curfew Row to its east end and turn right on to Charlotte Street. Follow this south to Bridge Lane and George

Street, and continue south to the High Street. Turn right, cross the High Street and head for St John's Kirk just south of the High Street on St John Street.

5 St John's Kirk
Perth's oldest building has stained glass and an elegant spire. Fiery Protestant John Knox preached in favour of Reformation of the Church here in 1559 – with unfortunate results for several of Perth's monastic foundations. *Follow St John Street south and continue*

down Princes Street. Turn left on to Marshall Place.

6 Fergusson Gallery
One of the leading members of the group of painters known as the Scottish Colourists, John Fergusson (1874–1961) worked mainly in France, but much of his vivid work was left to Perth and is now housed in a former water tower. *To return to your starting point, turn north up Tay Street and walk along the west bank of the Tay to the High Street.*

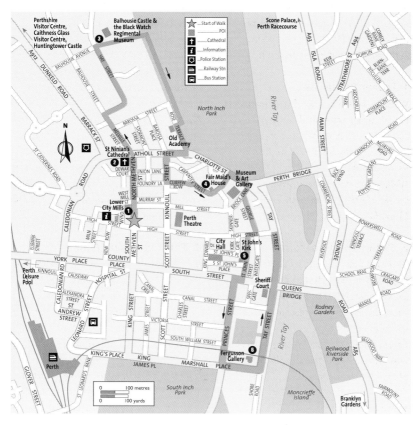

Pitlochry

Pitlochry owes its tourism popularity to its location on the main route into the Highlands. It's a handy stop on the way from Perth to Inverness, but it is also a convenient base for exploring Loch Tummel, Loch Rannoch and Rannoch Moor. Pitlochry has a plethora of places to stay, eat and drink, but few are outstanding, and some can be overpriced. The town can be very crowded in July and August. This said, it does have a few sights worth seeing – notably two interesting distilleries, and a pioneering ecotourism attraction.

Bell's Blair Athol Distillery

Founded in 1798, Blair Athol is still a working distillery and is located on the outskirts of Pitlochry (don't confuse it with Blair Atholl). It offers distillery tours, fascinating insights into the alchemy and science of malt whisky distilling, and of course an opportunity to sample and buy the finished product.

Perth Road, Pitlochry. Tel: (01796) 482 003. www.discovering-distilleries.com. Open: Apr–Oct Mon–Sat 9.30am– 5.30pm, Sun 10am–5pm. Tours: Nov–Mar Mon–Fri 11am, 1pm & 3pm.

Edradour Distillery

Edradour is Scotland's smallest distillery, and one of the oldest. Unlike most of its larger competitors, its guided tours are free and include a dram of Edradour's famous single malt. There is also a tasting bar and shop.

On the A924 from Pitlochry, past village of Moulin. Tel: (01796) 472 095. www.edradour.co.uk. Open: 3 Jan–end Feb Mon–Sat 10am–4pm, Sun noon–4pm; Mar–Oct Mon–Sat

The Edradour Distillery was established in 1825

The Queen's View, beloved of Queen Victoria

9.30am–6pm, Sun 11.30am–5pm;
Nov–Dec Mon–Sat 9.30am–4pm, Sun
11.30am–4pm. Last tour starts 1 hour
before closing. Closed: 25–26 Dec &
1–2 Jan. Free admission.

Killiecrankie Visitor Centre

The slopes of this narrow gorge of the
River Garry, where Viscount Dundee's
Highlanders won their famous victory
in 1689, are clad in oak, birch and ash
trees. It is a beautiful place in its own
right, but its history is brought to life
by an exhibition in the visitor centre,
which is run by the National Trust for
Scotland. Nearby is the 'Soldier's Leap',
where a fleeing redcoat is said to have
escaped the claymores of the clans by
jumping the gorge.
B8079, 4km (2½ miles) north of Pitlochry.
Tel: (0844) 493 2194. www.nts.org.
Battlefield site open all year daily.

Visitor centre open: 21 Mar–31 Oct daily
10am–5.30pm. Closed: 1 Nov–
20 Mar. Free admission.

Queen's View Visitor Centre

Looking out over Loch Tummel to the
slopes of Schiehallion, it is easy to see
why this is supposed to have been one
of Queen Victoria's favourite Scottish
views – hence its name. The visitor
centre has a free exhibition and
audiovisual presentation and there are
easy forest walks in the woods nearby.
Allean, Tay Forest Park, B8019, 10km
(6 miles) west of Pitlochry.
Tel: (01796) 473 123. www.forestry.gov.uk.
Open: Apr–mid-Nov daily 10am–6pm.
Closed: mid-Nov–Mar. Free admission.

Scottish Hydroelectric Visitor Centre

This pioneering attempt to merge the
interests of wildlife with the energy
needs of mankind opened in 1951; it
has become a blueprint for similar
ecotourism projects in Scotland and
around the world. Pitlochry's
hydroelectric dam project posed a
threat to salmon making their way
upriver to their spawning grounds in
Loch Faskally, above Pitlochry. The
solution was the 'salmon ladder' – 34
water-filled artificial pools, up which
the fish can swim and leap to reach
their destination. It is 310m (1,017ft)
long and was the first of its kind in
the world. Up to 5,000 salmon use
the ladder each year between April
and October on their annual
spawning run.

Pitlochry Power Station. Tel: (01796) 473 152. www.scottish-southern.co.uk. Open: Apr–Jun & Sept–Oct Mon–Fri 10am–5.30pm; Jul–Aug daily 10am–5.30pm. Closed: Nov–Mar. Free admission.

Rannoch Moor

Wild and windswept Rannoch Moor, with its rolling landscapes of peat bog, heather moor and ancient woodland, feels wonderfully remote and inaccessible. It is not, indeed, very easy to get to by car – but Rannoch Station, which appears to be the loneliest railway station in Britain, in fact has four trains a day from Glasgow and an overnight sleeper direct from London, so it is not as desolate as it seems. There are few places in Britain where you can get so far from civilisation: the A82 road to Fort William crosses the moor

Castle McDuck, the ancestral home of Donald Duck's miserly Scottish relative, Scrooge McDuck, is said to be located in 'Dismal Downs', somewhere on Rannoch Moor.

before plunging into Glencoe to the north, but the only way of crossing from east to west is on foot. Rannoch Moor covers an area of around 130sq km (50sq miles) and is some 16km (10 miles) across; it forms a rolling plateau, hemmed in by rugged peaks. This is a watery landscape, spattered with little lochans and larger lochs, including Loch Rannoch, which forms its southern boundary, and is linked by a myriad of fast-flowing, peat-tinted streams. For the energetic, it is prime walking country. A section of the West Highland Way walking trail crosses the moor from south to north, then continues on into Glencoe. At the

Buachaille Etive Mor at the north end of Rannoch Moor

THE SCHIEHALLION EXPERIMENT

In 1774, the British astronomer-royal, Nevil Maskelyne, chose Schiehallion as the site of the first attempt to calculate the mass of the Earth by measuring the displacement of a pendulum. Maskelyne chose the mountain because of its isolation – to minimise interference with his pendulum by man-made vibrations – and because of its symmetrical, conical shape. His original experiment was repeated in 2005, with remarkably similar results.

northern end of the moor, Buachaille Etive Mor (the Great Shepherd of Etive) is a prominent landmark at the mouth of Glen Etive.

Rannoch Moor also has pockets of what is believed to be the oldest deciduous woodland in Scotland. This consists of mixed patches of oak, ash, rowan and birch, and is supposed typical of the woodland that originally cloaked much of the Highlands. It is also noted for its wildlife. Walkers may see buzzards, golden eagles and red deer. Its rarer plants and insects are a bit less exciting (except to specialists): the Rannoch rush, which is found nowhere else, is an unassuming, brownish plant, and the endemic narrow-headed ant (*Formica exsecta*) is equally unpretentious.

Schiehallion

The lonely, almost perfectly conical peak of Schiehallion is one of the most spectacular and magical mountains in the Perthshire Highlands. Its name may mean 'Holy place of the Sidhe' – the fairy folk who were both feared and venerated by the ancient Caledonians – and it still has an aura of mystery about it. Traditionally, girls from nearby villages visited the Maiden's Well, a spring on the east flank of the hill, every May Day to dance and drink its water, a tradition that was almost certainly a fertility ritual carried on from pre-Christian times. With a height of 1,083m (3,553ft) above sea level, Schiehallion easily qualifies as one of the higher Munros, but the ascent is quite gentle and its accessibility makes it a popular climb, attracting up to 20,000 people a year. The mountain is part-owned by the conservation organisation the John Muir Trust. Because of its location, it is sometimes cited as the exact geographical centre of Scotland, which adds to its mystique.

The conical mountain of Schiehallion

The Perthshire Highlands

The Highland Regiments

Fully armed, the clan warrior was a fearsome sight. The clansman's main weapon was the basket-hilted broadsword – also known as the claymore – carried on the right hip. He wore a small, round shield or *targe* on his left arm. His other edged weapons included the dirk – something between a very long dagger and a very short sword – for fighting at close quarters, and the *sgian dubh* or black knife. With the advent of gunpowder, the clan warrior added a flintlock musket and a bandolier stuffed with ornate silver pistols to his arsenal. Poorer clansmen carried the fearsome (but clumsy)

Battle re-enactment at Glencoe

long-handled Lochaber axe. The full 'Highland charge' with broadsword, dirk, *targe* and axe shattered Lowland and English armies on more than one occasion, notably at Killiecrankie, near Pitlochry, in 1689, and at Prestonpans and Falkirk in 1745. Ironically, the Highland Host at Killiecrankie was led by a Lowland Jacobite, Viscount Graham of Claverhouse (who was killed in his moment of victory), while the Williamite Lowlanders on the other side were commanded by a Highlander, Hugh Mackay of Scourie. But the Highland charge ultimately met its match in the form of disciplined ranks of redcoats with musket and fixed bayonets. A few days after Killiecrankie, Claverhouse's Highlanders were stopped in their tracks by the muskets of the Cameronians at Dunkeld, and the victories of 1745 ended with the debacle of Culloden.

After Culloden, the Highlands surprisingly quickly became a fertile recruiting ground for the British Army, and clans who had once been a thorn in the government's side were marshalled into the kilted regiments that became the shock troops of the British Empire. General Wolfe, who as

The Highlanders Regimental Museum at Fort George near Inverness

a loyalist officer had fought the rebels at Culloden, a few years later led men from those same clans to victory against the French at Québec. Highlanders were the elite infantry of Wellington's armies in India, in Spain and at Waterloo. During the Crimean War, they formed the 'thin red line' that outfought the Russians at Balaclava. During World War I, their peculiar uniform and legendary ferocity led their German opponents to nickname them 'the Ladies from Hell', and during World War II they served with equal distinction in Montgomery's 8th Army in North Africa and Italy. The 51st Highland Division was the last British force to resist the German invasion of France in 1940, finally being forced to lay down its arms two weeks after the rest of the British Expeditionary Force had been evacuated from Dunkirk.

Not all tartan-wearing regiments came from the Highlands. The oldest of them all, the Black Watch (so called because of its dark regimental tartan), was raised from the Lowlands to police the Highland Line and was garrisoned in Perth. The Lowland sharpshooters who stopped the Highland Host at Dunkeld later formed the Cameronian regiment, named after their fiery Presbyterian leader, Richard Cameron. The Seaforths and the Gordons were both drawn from the farmlands of the northeast, and the Highland Light Infantry's main recruiting ground was working-class Glasgow. Perhaps the most famous of the regiments drawn from the Highland heartlands was the Argyll and Sutherland Highlanders, recruited from the lands of the Clan Campbell, and traditionally officered by the sons of Campbell chieftains.

The Grampian Highlands and Cairngorms

Rising steeply from the gentler farmlands of Perthshire and Strathmore, the Grampian Highlands are immediately impressive. At the heart of this mountainous region is the 'pocket wilderness' of the Cairngorms National Park, offering some of the finest hillwalking and mountain scenery in Britain. On the fringes of the Grampian massif are the gentler landscapes of Strathspey and Royal Deeside.

Aviemore

Aviemore is a purpose-built resort that acts as a base for a wide range of outdoor activities including skiing and tobogganing, walking and climbing, canoeing, river rafting and golf.

Cairngorm Mountain Railway

The highest and fastest funicular railway in Britain runs from Aviemore to the Cairn Gorm ski area, close to the summit of Cairn Gorm, the UK's sixth-highest mountain. At the top, there are some of Scotland's best ski pistes and toboggan runs, superb panoramic views, bars, a restaurant, exhibition and shop. *Aviemore. Tel: (01479) 861 261. www.cairngormmountain.com. Open: daily. First train up 9am (Wed 9.20am), last train down 4.30pm (5.00pm in summer) – see website or ring for timetables. Admission charge.*

Cairngorm Reindeer Centre

The Cairngorm Reindeer Centre's herd graze freely on the hillsides above Glenmore and can be visited in their natural environment.
Reindeer House, Glenmore, on the B970, 9.6km (6 miles) from Aviemore. Tel: (01479) 861 228. www.cairngormreindeer.co.uk. Open: daily 10am–5pm. Closed: 25 Dec & 1 Jan. Visit to the herd May–Sept daily 11am & 2.30pm; Oct–Apr daily 11am. Admission charge.

Rothiemurchus Estate

On the northern edge of the Cairngorms National Park, Rothiemurchus has been the private estate of the Grant family for more than 400 years. It now offers a range of activities, including pony trekking, quad-bike riding, mountain biking, canoeing, 4WD tours, wildlife watching, canoeing, archery and clay shooting, and visits to the estate's own loch, Loch an Eilein, and its island castle.
Rothiemurchus Centre, Inverdruie, by Aviemore. Tel: (01479) 812 345. www.rothiemurchus.net. Open: Feb–Oct daily 9.30am–5.30pm. Closed: Nov–Jan.

Strathspey Steam Railway

This private railway line runs from Aviemore across rolling moorland, then heads through the winding valley of the River Spey to Boat of Garten, Broomhill and Grantown-on-Spey. The latest addition to the trains preserved and restored by the Strathspey Railway Association is the pretty blue-liveried ex-Caledonian Railway steam locomotive No 828, the last of its kind.

Aviemore Station, Aviemore. Tel: (01479) 810 725. www.strathspeyrailway.co.uk – see website or ring for train timetable. Admission charge.

Ballater

Ballater is a small and pleasant market town that owes most of its tourism appeal to the reputation of nearby Balmoral Castle, summer home of the British royals and their guests.

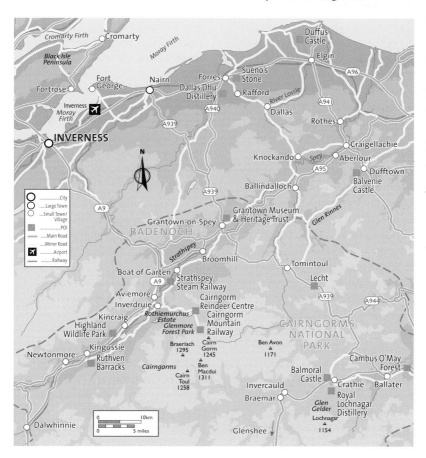

The main street in Ballater

Balmoral Castle

This unique Scottish baronial pile has been the Highland holiday residence of the British Royal Family since 1852, when Prince Albert, the Prince Consort, bought the estate as a gift for Queen Victoria. The queen had first visited the estate in 1848. Albert, together with the Aberdeen architect William Smith, designed a palatial new castle, which was built on the site of an earlier castle and was completed in 1856. Balmoral is built of pale granite, quarried from nearby Glen Gelder, giving it a fairy-tale appearance that is less forbidding than most Highland castles. The castle is surrounded by a 20,235-hectare (50,000-acre) estate and is overlooked by the peak of Lochnagar, which stands in the heart of the Cairngorms National Park. Within, in the castle's ballroom, a collection of portraits and landscapes is on display to the visiting public, but the other rooms remain off-limits. Admission charges include access to the gardens, a wildlife exhibition, and other exhibitions including a collection of carriages used by the Royal Family on the estate.

Crathie, A93, 13km (8 miles) west of Ballater. Tel: (01339) 742 354. www.balmoralcastle.com. Open: end Mar–Jul daily 10am–5pm. Last admission 4pm. Closed: Aug–end Mar. Admission charge.

Cambus O'May Forest

This slice of managed woodland just outside Ballater and just off the main road is a great place for a breath of fresh air, a stroll or a picnic in the woods when travelling through Deeside. There is a picnic area and four signposted walks leading to a scenic viewpoint and two small woodland lochs.

A93, 4km (2¹/₂ miles) east of Ballater. No tel. www.forestry.gov.uk. See website for times of ranger-guided walks and other events, for which there is a charge.

Old Royal Station

A full-scale replica of the royal carriage used by Queen Victoria and her brood when they travelled to Balmoral sits outside this restored 19th-century railway station. Inside, there is a lavishly appointed royal waiting room built specially for Queen Victoria, and an exhibition of photos, uniforms and other railway paraphernalia from the station's golden age.

Station Square, Ballater. Tel: (01339) 755
306. www.aberdeen-grampian.com.
Open: Jun & Sept daily 9am–6pm;
Jul–Aug daily 9.30am–7pm; Oct–May
daily 10am–6pm. Free admission.

Royal Lochnagar Distillery

Shiny copper stills and huge mash tuns
line the walls of this historic distillery,
which stands right next to Balmoral
Castle. Royal Lochnagar is the smallest
of the many Scottish distilleries owned
by the drinks giant Diageo, employing
six skilled distillers and producing a
renowned 12-year-old single malt
whisky. The price of the guided tour
includes a free dram, and the distillery
also offers tutored whisky tastings.
Crathie, A93, 13km (8 miles) west of
Ballater. Tel: (01339) 742 700.
www.discovering-distilleries.com.

Open: Jan–Feb Mon–Fri 10am–4pm; Mar
& Nov–Dec Mon–Sat 10am–4pm;
Apr–Oct Mon–Sat 10am–5pm, Sun
11.30am–5pm. Admission charge.

Braemar

Like nearby Ballater, Braemar is a
hotbed of tartan tourism that reaches
its peak during the annual Royal
Braemar Gathering, when thousands
flock to see Highland dancers, pipers
and heavyweight sportsmen
performing (*see p25*). The small but
still formidable-looking Braemar
Castle was garrisoned by government
troops until 1831 and has been
restored by volunteers.
Braemar Castle. No tel.
www.braemarscotland.co.uk.
Open: May–Oct Sat–Sun 11am–4pm.
Closed: Nov–Apr. Admission charge.

The Grampian Highlands and Cairngorms

The Royal Lochnagar Distillery, established in 1845

Balmoral and the Royals

Balmoral Castle has been the home of the British Royal Family in Scotland since 1852, when the Prince Consort, Prince Albert, bought the original 15th-century castle and its estates for Queen Victoria. Albert – very much a 'hands-on' consort – took a major part in laying out the grand gardens that surround Balmoral, and also participated in the design of the new castle, which probably accounts for its distinctly Germanic style. Completed in 1856, Balmoral spawned a wave of imitative buildings and grand houses in the Scottish baronial style. Victoria loved spending time at Balmoral, where she could escape for a while from the concerns of ruling her ever-expanding empire.

Like most members of the ruling classes of 19th-century Europe, Albert enjoyed the manly pastimes of hunting and shooting. His locally born ghillie (a ghillie is a mountain guide

Balmoral Castle and the River Dee, looking west towards Braemar

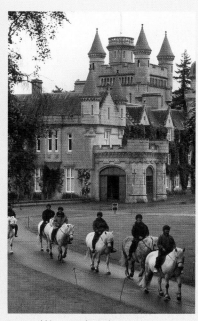

Pony trekking at Balmoral

56, almost as much as she mourned Albert's. When he succeeded to the throne on Victoria's death, Edward and his cronies made every effort to expunge all traces of Brown from Balmoral, destroying photographs of Brown with the queen and removing the statue that she had erected in his memory to a remote corner of the estate.

Later British royals have been equally fond of Balmoral. Queen Elizabeth II and her family stay at the castle for several weeks each summer, and both the Duke of Edinburgh and the Prince of Wales are as keen on shooting, fishing and deer stalking on the royal estates as was their ancestor Prince Albert. Prince Charles wrote and illustrated a children's book, *The Old Man of Lochnagar*, for his sons Prince William and Prince Harry when they were small boys holidaying at Balmoral, though as young men both princes appear to prefer the fashionable clubs of the London scene to the rustic surroundings of Royal Deeside. Perhaps they have been influenced by their mother, the late Diana, Princess of Wales, who reportedly found Balmoral cold, gloomy and depressing – in stark contrast to Queen Victoria, who regarded Balmoral as 'my dear paradise in the Highlands'.

and proficient deer stalker), John Brown, became the queen's personal servant, and after Prince Albert's early death in 1861, Brown became perhaps her closest confidant and comforter. As a mere commoner, he was resented by many of the queen's courtiers – and by her heir, Edward, later King Edward VII – and there were even rumours that the queen's relationship with Brown was far too close to be respectable. Whether their relationship was ever more than platonic is debatable, but the queen certainly seems to have mourned Brown's death in 1883, at the age of

Auld Brig of Dee
(Old Invercauld Bridge)

The 'auld brig' (old bridge) across the River Dee at Invercauld must be one of the best-known icons of Deeside. Built in 1852, it is depicted on dozens (if not hundreds) of postcards and calendars and landscape paintings.

Invercauld, 5km (3 miles) east of Braemar.

Braemar Highland Heritage Centre

The Highland Heritage Centre celebrates tartan and tradition with displays of Highland dress, an audiovisual presentation focusing on Braemar's history and its links with the Royal Family, and a shop packed with all manner of Highland souvenirs.

WHAT'S A MUNRO?

A Munro is a Scottish mountain more than 3,000ft (914.4m) in height. The Munros owe their name to the mountaineer and surveyor Sir Hugh Munro (1856–1919), who compiled the first list of such peaks in 1891. There are 284 Munros, all of which are in the Highlands.

The Mews, Invercauld Road, Braemar. Tel: (01339) 741 944. Open: Apr–Sept daily 9am–5.30pm; Oct–Mar daily 9.30am–4.30pm. Free admission.

Cairngorms National Park

Britain's largest wilderness area was declared a national park in 2003 and comprises an area of 3,800sq km (1,467sq miles). It stretches from the

Loch Morlich at Glenmore, in the heart of the Cairngorms

Spey valley in the north to the heads of the Angus glens in the south, and from Ballater on Deeside to Dalwhinnie in the west. Within it, above the 600m (1,970ft) contour line, lies the largest area of arctic mountain landscape in the UK. The park is home to many of Britain's rarest plant, bird and animal species, including red deer, golden eagle, osprey, Scottish crossbill, wild cat, pine marten, capercaillie and ptarmigan, as well as to 16,000 people – a population density of just 4.2 people per square kilometre, though that is boosted by up to 500,000 visitors every year.

The Cairngorms is an area of great beauty and great environmental diversity, from heather moorland and harsh rocky uplands to gentler valleys carved out by Ice Age glaciation. This wild but easily accessible landscape is very popular hillwalking territory, with four of Scotland's five highest mountains, several Munros and no fewer than seven summits more than 1,100m (3,610ft) in height, including Lochnagar (1,154m/3,787ft), Ben Avon (1,171m/ 3,843ft), Cairn Toul (1,258m/4,128ft), Braeriach (1,295m/4,250ft), Ben Macdui (1,311m/4,302ft) and Cairn Gorm itself (1,245m/4,086ft).
Road access: A93 from Perth, Braemar or Ballater. A939 from Grantown-on-Spey or Ballater. A9 from Inverness. Most of the national park is accessible only on foot. Cairngorms National Park Authority, 14 The Square, Grantown-on-Spey PH26 3HG. Tel: (01479) 873 535. www.cairngorms.co.uk

Dalwhinnie

Dalwhinnie, set in a pass on the A9 highway 320m (1,050ft) above sea level, is a small village that is best known for its distillery, which is sometimes claimed to be the highest in Scotland. Its name means 'meeting place', and cattle drovers from the north and west Highlands would rendezvous here before driving their herds south to the Lowland cattle markets of Falkirk and Crieff.
A9, 64km (40 miles) south of Inverness.

Dalwhinnie Distillery Visitor Centre

Now owned by the Diageo company, Dalwhinnie produces a renowned single malt whisky from the snowmelt of the Allt an t'Sluic stream. The distillery tour lets visitors see distillers at work and sample the final product. *Dalwhinnie. Tel: (01540) 672 219. www.diageo.com. Open: Feb–Easter & Nov–Dec Mon–Fri 11am–2pm; Easter– Apr Mon–Fri 9.30am–5pm; May–Sept Mon–Sat 9.30am–5pm, Sun (Jul–Aug) 11am–4pm; Oct Mon–Sat 10am–5pm. Closed: Jan. Admission charge.*

Duffus Castle

A water-filled moat surrounds the roadside ruins of one of the earliest Norman motte-and-bailey castles in Scotland, built during the 13th and 14th centuries by the de Moravia barons, later known as the Murray family, who eventually became dukes of Sutherland and Atholl. They lent their name to this entire region of northern Scotland, which is still known as Moray.

B9012, 8km (5 miles) northwest of Elgin
town centre. Tel: (01667) 460 232.
www.historic-scotland.gov.uk.
Open: daily, dawn until dusk.
Free admission.

Elgin

Straddling the River Lossie, less than
8km (5 miles) from the shore of the
Moray Firth, Elgin is a historic town
with a turbulent history, surrounding
the impressive ruins of a 13th-century
cathedral. The town was razed to the
ground by Robert Stewart, the 'Wolf of
Badenoch', in 1390, and most of its
sturdy and attractive buildings date
from the 18th and 19th centuries.

Biblical Garden

This eccentric but oddly appealing
1.2-hectare (3-acre) garden is reckoned
to have a sample of each plant
mentioned in the Bible – there's even a
patch of sand and gravel to represent
Sinai, and a miniature grotto stands in
for the Cave of the Resurrection. Life-
size tableaux of biblical figures are
dotted around the garden.
Cooper Park, King Street, Elgin.
www.biblicalgardenelgin.com.
Open: May–Sept daily 10am–7.30pm.
Closed: Oct–Apr. Free admission.

Elgin Cathedral

The ruins of Elgin's fine cathedral,
founded in 1224, are among the most
evocative in all of northern Scotland.
The cathedral was set on fire in 1390
by Robert Stewart, after the bishop
of Elgin had the temerity to criticise
his promiscuity. It was rebuilt,
but damaged again during the
Reformation, after which it fell once
more into ruin. Inside the shell of the
choir is a stone slab marked with
cryptic Pictish symbols.

Elgin Cathedral is known locally as the 'lantern of the north'

Elgin town centre. Tel: (01343) 547 171.
www.historic-scotland.gov.uk.
Open: Apr–Oct daily 9.30am–5.30pm;
Nov–Mar Sat–Wed 9.30am–4.30pm.
Admission charge.

Elgin Museum
This independently run museum is best
known for its considerable collection of
Pictish stones, carved with sinuous
patterns and enigmatic symbols, the
meaning of which has been lost in the
mists of time. It also has an interesting
collection of local fossils.
1 High Street, Elgin. Tel: (01343) 543 675.
www.elginmuseum.org.uk.
Open: Apr–Oct Mon–Fri 10am–5pm,
Sat 11am–4pm. Closed: Nov–Mar & Sun.
Admission charge.

Forres
Benromach Distillery and
Malt Whisky Centre
Benromach is the region's smallest
distillery. It reopened in 1998 after being
closed for several years, so its product
still has some ageing to do; HRH the
Prince of Wales is reportedly a fan.
Invererne Road, off the A96, 500m
(550 yards) from Forres town centre.
Tel: (01309) 675 968.
www.benromach.com. Open: May–Sept
Mon–Sat 9.30am–5pm, Sun (Jun–Aug)
noon–6pm; Oct–Apr Mon–Fri 10am–
4pm. Admission charge.

Dallas Dhu Distillery
This small distillery opened in 1898
and has a visitor centre and an

audiovisual presentation on the making
of Scotch whisky and the traditions
that surround it.
Mannachie Road, Forres, 1.5km (1 mile)
south of Forres. Tel: (01309) 676 548.
Open: Apr–Sept daily 9.30am–6.30pm;
Oct–Mar Sat–Wed 9.30am–4.30pm.
Admission charge.

Sueno's Stone
This remarkable monolith, carved from
top to bottom with intricate interlocking
patterns, is regarded as the most
important ancient symbol-stone in
Britain. More than 6m (20ft) in height,
it is now cased in shockproof and
weatherproof glass to protect it from
erosion and from the local graffiti
artists. It is believed to be a memorial
stone, erected around AD 1000.
East roundabout, Forres.
Tel: (01667) 460 232. www.historic-
scotland.gov.uk

Glenshee
Dotted with the ruins of old shielings,
Glen Shee (from the Gaelic *Gleann*
Sidhe, or 'Glen of the Fairies') forms the
main route between the lowlands of
Perthshire and Braemar on Deeside,
carrying the A93 – the highest public
road in Scotland – across the mountains
by the steep and winding 'Devil's Elbow'
and the Cairnwell pass, 665m (2,182ft)
above sea level and 80km (50 miles)
northeast of Perth. This is also where
skiing in Scotland was born, and it is
regarded as one of Scotland's favourite
ski areas.

Conservation areas at Corrie Fee and Caenlochan provide refuge for some of the largest flocks of ptarmigan in Scotland, and red grouse, mountain hare, golden plover, ring ouzel, snow bunting and golden eagle also breed in the area. There is a magnificent panoramic view of the whole massif of the Cairngorms from Cairnwell.

Glenshee Ski Centre
With 36 runs and 21 lifts and tows connecting three valleys and four mountains, this is the UK's largest ski centre and is also popular with snowboarders. A plastic 'dry ski' slope makes practice possible even when snow conditions are poor.
Cairnwell, 15km (9 miles) south of Braemar. Tel: (01339) 741 320. www.ski-glenshee.co.uk. Open: daily 8.30am–5pm during ski season (normally late Dec–early Apr but can be as late as end May). See website or telephone for snow conditions. Admission charge.

Kingussie
Kingussie (pronounced 'Kin-yoosie'), on the River Spey, is a small town with a dual history. The first settlement in the region grew up on the opposite bank of the river, around Ruthven Castle, seat of the Stewart lords of Badenoch, but Kingussie is a much more modern creation. The building of new roads and bridges in the 19th century made it a more important place, and the advent of the Perth–Inverness railway line in 1863 transformed it into a popular resort town. Its streets are lined with attractive 19th-century villas.
B9512, 11km (7 miles) south of Aviemore.

Icy waters at the Spittal of Glenshee

Highland Folk Museum

This lively, fascinating little open-air museum takes the visitor back in time with exhibits including a traditional 'black house' from the Isle of Lewis, farming and weaving equipment, costumes, musical instruments, furniture and a special exhibition on the history of Highland travelling people.
Duke Street, Kingussie.
Tel: (01540) 673 551.
www.highlandfolk.com. Open: Apr–Aug Mon–Sat 10am–5pm; Sept–Oct Mon–Fri 10am–4pm. Closed: Nov–Mar. Free admission.

Highland Wildlife Park

Run by the Royal Zoological Society of Scotland, this open-air zoo features themed habitats that can be explored on foot as well as safari-style trips in the main reserve. Animals and birds on view include Highland species such as wild cat, otter and capercaillie, and the zoo also has a collection of animals that were native to Scotland but are now extinct, including wolves, beaver, lynx and bison.
Kincraig, Kingussie. Tel: (01540) 651 270. www.highlandwildlifepark.org. Open: Apr–May & Sept–Oct daily 10am–6pm; Jun–Aug daily 10am–7pm; Nov–Mar daily 10am–4pm. Admission charge.

Ruthven Barracks

The imposing ruined shell of Ruthven Barracks stands atop a grassy knoll that might well have been the site of a series of strongholds dating back to Iron Age times. It commands a strategic crossing

A Scottish wildcat at the Highland Wildlife Park

of the River Spey, and a castle stood here as early as 1229. In the 14th and 15th centuries it was a stronghold of the Stewart lords of Badenoch. It was severely damaged during the Cromwellian invasion and the Jacobite troubles of 1689 and 1715, and after the 1715 rising it was rebuilt as a garrison stronghold for government troops. It was finally reduced to a ruin by Charles Edward Stuart's Jacobites as they retreated north in 1746.
B970, 1.5km (1 mile) south of Kingussie centre. Tel: (01667) 460 232. Open: daily, dawn until dusk. Free admission.

Newtonmore

Like neighbouring Kingussie, Newtonmore is really a recent creation, by Highland standards. It owes much of its growth to the construction of proper highways through the region in the early 19th century. At the same time, its population was boosted by large numbers of people evicted from their land during the infamous 'Clearances' (*see pp16–17*). Reminders of their vanished lifestyle can be seen at the Newtonmore annexe of the Highland Folk Museum. Sightseeing aside, Newtonmore has a reasonable choice of places to stay, eat and drink, making it a convenient stop.

A86, 4km (2½ miles) west of Kingussie.

Clan Macpherson Museum

This small but attractive museum tells the story of the clan way of life and especially of the Macphersons of the Badenoch region, with clan relics, tartans, maps and prints.

Main Street, Newtonmore. Tel: (01540) 673 332. www.clan-macpherson.org. Open: Apr–Oct Mon–Sat 10am–5pm, Sun noon–5pm. Closed: Nov–Mar. Free admission.

Highland Folk Museum

The Newtonmore branch of the Highland Folk Museum in Kingussie (*see p57*) has a range of traditional

Balvenie Castle in Dufftown

buildings and other outdoor exhibits laid out in a mile-long site that includes an 18th-century township and a working farm using methods and equipment from the 1940s. It is staffed by costumed interpreters who bring the past to life for the visitor.

Aultairie Croft, Newtonmore. Tel: (01540) 661 307. Open: Apr–Aug daily 10.30am–5.30pm; Sept daily 11am–4.30pm; Oct Mon–Fri 11am–4.30pm. Closed: Nov–Mar. Admission charge.

Waltzing Waters

This high-tech show claims to be the world's most elaborate water, light and music production. It certainly makes a change from the diet of history, heritage and ecotourism that prevails in this part of the world, with its dazzling display of computer-synchronised, colourfully lit fountains.

Balavil Brae, Newtonmore. Tel: (01540) 673 752. www.waltzingwaters.co.uk. Open: early Feb–mid-Dec daily, shows hourly 10am–4pm (show lasts 40 mins); additional evening shows (Jul–Aug) at 8.30pm. Closed: mid-Dec–early Feb. Admission charge.

Speyside
Balvenie Castle

Although it is much ruined, Balvenie is still well worth a look and is rich in history. Built in the 13th century by the Comyn lords, its guests have included Edward I of England in 1304 and Mary, Queen of Scots, in 1562. Cumberland's

Grantown-on-Spey was once the capital of the region

troopers occupied it in 1746, after Culloden, and it is now little more than a picturesque shell.

Dufftown, A941, 25km (16 miles) southeast of Elgin. Tel: (01340) 820 121. Open: Apr–Sept daily 9.30am–6.30pm. Closed: Oct–Mar. Admission charge.

Grantown Museum and Heritage Trust

Grantown-on-Spey is the largest village in Strathspey and is the region's original 'capital'. With a population of just over 2,000, it is really a large village rather than a town, but with its neatly laid-out streets it is a fine example of one of the planned settlements designed at the behest of forward-looking landowners during the 18th century.

The museum, housed in a former school, tells the story of the planning and building of Grantown-on-Spey by Sir James Grant, the local bigwig whose vision was to create one of the first planned towns in the Highlands.

Burnfield House, Burnfield Avenue, Grantown-on-Spey. Tel: (01479) 872 478. www.grantownmuseum.co.uk. Open: Mar–end Oct Mon–Fri 10am–4pm. Closed: end Oct–Feb & Sat–Sun. Admission charge.

Speyside's distilleries
Aberlour Distillery Visitor Centre

Aberlour offers an educational and entertaining introduction to the world of malt whisky, sniffing and tasting the new distillate before it begins ageing, then comparing the raw spirit with five of the distillery's fine single malts.

Aberlour Distillery, Aberlour, 35km (22 miles) northeast of Grantown-on-
(Cont. on p62)

Scotch whisky: the water of life

Think of the Scottish Highlands and you think of Scotch whisky – or, in Gaelic, *uisghe beatha*, which means 'the water of life'. As Scotland's national bard, Robert Burns, wrote: 'Whisky and freedom gang the gither; tak aff your dram' ('Whisky and freedom go together; drink your measure').

In fact, Irish monks might have a better claim than the Scots to have invented the stuff, and the technology of distilling was – ironically – well known to the teetotal Muslim Arab world long before it reached the remote islands of Britain and Ireland. The Arabs used distillation to make perfumes and essential oils from flowers, and from fruit such as oranges and lemons, and nuts such as almonds. The Scots have been putting the technique to another use since around the 15th century.

Whisky is made by the process of malting, in which germinating barley grains are lightly toasted, then left to ferment in large vats to create the basic 'wash' – a beer-like liquid from

Cardhu Distillery makes one of the most famous blended whiskies, Johnny Walker

which the raw alcohol that eventually becomes whisky will be distilled in huge copper pot-stills.

After being distilled several times to remove all impurities, the raw distillate is left to age for several years in oak casks. Traditionally, casks that had already been used to store sherry were used, and the casks added colour and complex flavours to the spirit. Today, many distillers have taken to experimenting with casks that have held other wines such as Chardonnay, creating new styles of whisky. Whisky may be aged for 5, 10, 12 years or even more, but it's questionable whether ageing more than 20 years adds any extra dimension to the drink. Before bottling, the whisky is diluted from its ferociously potent 'cask strength' – close to 100 per cent alcohol – with clear spring water, bringing the alcohol content down to around 40 per cent.

To qualify as a 'single malt', a whisky must be made only from spirit distilled from malted barley, and real purists might argue that the barley itself should be grown in Scotland. Blended whiskies are made by combining a proportion of single malt with neutral grain spirit; generally speaking, the higher the proportion of malt to grain, the higher the quality of the blend. Such whiskies are made as far from Scotland as Japan, Argentina and India, as well as in Scotland itself. Prestige blends command high prices in overseas markets such as mainland Europe, Asia and the US, but few Scots regard them as comparable with a good single malt.

Whisky is made all over Scotland, in the Lowlands and the Northern and Western Isles as well as on Speyside, but more than half of Scotland's single malt distilleries – 46 in all – are on the banks of the Spey and its tributaries. Light in colour and body, somewhat sweet in flavour and less peaty and smoky than the darker malts from the island distilleries of Islay and Jura, they are easy to drink and are the perfect introduction to malt whisky. Glenlivet, perhaps the most famous of them all, was already well known as early as the 18th century, even though it was being distilled illicitly at the time. The Scottish Parliament, spotting a useful source of revenue, first taxed whisky in the 17th century, and many distillers took to conducting their operations in secret to evade the tax. Taxation has risen steadily ever since – about 90 per cent of what you pay for a bottle of whisky goes straight into the government's pocket – but illicit distilling is no longer big business in the Highlands.

Spey on the A95. Tel: (01340) 832 157. www.aberlour.co.uk. Tours: Mar–Oct Mon–Sat 10.30am & 2pm, Sun 11.30am & 3pm; Nov–mid-Dec Mon–Fri 10.30am. Closed: mid-Dec–Feb. Admission charge.

Cardhu Distillery Visitor Centre

Cardhu made whisky on the quiet for many years before it went legitimate as a licensed distillery in 1824. It makes its own single malt, and its malt whisky is also a key ingredient in Johnny Walker, one of the world's best-known blended whiskies.

Knockando, near Aberlour, 27km (17 miles) northeast of Grantown-on-Spey on the B9102. Tel: (01340) 872 555. Tours: Jan–Easter & Oct–Dec Mon–Fri 11am, 1pm & 2pm. Open: Easter–Jun Mon–Fri 10am–5pm; Jul–Sept Mon–Sat 10am–5pm, Sun noon–4pm. Admission charge.

Glen Grant Distillery and Garden In 1872, the famous Victorian explorer Major James Grant returned home from his travels in Africa and India to take over the distillery founded by his father and uncle in 1840. He laid out a beautiful woodland garden – perhaps to celebrate the fact that he was no longer in the steaming tropics but home in Scotland – which makes a pleasant place for a stroll after a visit to the distillery.

Rothes, A941, 16km (10 miles) south of Elgin. Tel: (01340) 832 118. Open: Apr–Oct Mon–Sat 10am–4pm, Sun 12.30–4pm. Closed: Nov–Mar. Free admission.

Glenfarclas Distillery One of the very few independent distilleries left in Scotland (most are now owned by large multinational companies), Glenfarclas has been run by the Grant family since 1865, when it was bought by John

The tranquil setting of Glenlivet Distillery

Grant, great-great-grandfather of the present owner, for the princely sum of £511 19s 0d.

Glenfarclas Road End, A95, 6.4km (4 miles) west of Aberlour. Tel: (01807) 500 257. www.glenfarclas.co.uk. Open: Apr–Jun Mon–Fri 10am–5pm; Jul–Sept Mon–Fri 10am–5pm, Sat 10am–4pm; Oct–Mar Mon–Fri 10am–4pm. Admission charge.

Glenfiddich Distillery Glenfiddich is one of the best-known Speyside malt whiskies, and has been made here since 1887. It is also the only Highland malt that has the distinction of being distilled, aged and bottled all at its own distillery. The free tour includes a look round the distillery and bottling hall and a free sample; the distillery also offers, for a fee, a connoisseur's tour, which includes a tutored 'nosing' and whisky-tasting session.

Dufftown, A941, 500m (550 yards) north of village centre. Tel: (01340) 820 373. www.glenfiddich.com. Open: Jan–Easter & Nov–Dec Mon–Fri 9.30am–4.30pm; Easter–Oct Mon–Sat 9.30am–4.30pm, Sun noon–4.30pm. Free admission.

Glenlivet Distillery Glenlivet, in the pretty glen of the same name, is almost synonymous with Speyside malts. The visitor centre focuses on the history of the label and the glen, with an audiovisual presentation, guided distillery tour and a sample dram. *Glenlivet, 16km (10 miles) north of Tomintoul. Tel: (01340) 821 720.*

The still room of the Glenfiddich Distillery

www.theglenlivet.com. Open: Apr–Oct Mon–Sat 10am–4pm, Sun 12.30–4pm. Closed: Nov–Mar. Free admission.

Tomintoul

Tomintoul's claim to fame is that it is the highest village in Scotland. That said, there is not a lot to detain you here except for its small museum.

Tomintoul Museum and Visitor Centre

The museum re-creates the interior and kitchen of a crofter's primitive cottage and the working space of a village smithy, and also features some displays on local wildlife, including the Scottish wildcat.

The Square, Tomintoul. Tel: (01309) 673 701. Open: Apr–Oct daily 9am–5pm. Closed: Nov–Mar. Free admission.

Drive: Speyside's distilleries

Speyside (or Strathspey), the home of Highland malt whisky, is a pretty region of tidy farmland, woods and villages scattered either side of the silvery River Spey, whose tributary streams provide the water to make some of the world's most famous malt whiskies. Many of Speyside's 40 or more distilleries are industrialised, but plenty offer a welcome and a complimentary dram to visitors.

Distance: 80km (50 miles). Allow 6 hours.

Leave Forres town centre by the A940 southbound and after approximately 800m (½ mile), take the first left, Mannachie Road, and drive 800m (½ mile) south.

1 Dallas Dhu Distillery

This small distillery, which opened in 1898, is the last of the 'old-style' distilleries. Inside is a visitor centre with multilingual audio tours, ending with a free sip.

Return to Forres, turn right (east) through the town centre, then leave Forres by the B9010 southbound, signposted to Rafford. After 12.5km (7¾ miles), turn right to Dallas. Drive through the village and take the first left. Continue south for 11km (7 miles). On reaching the larger B9102, turn left to Cardow and follow the signs to the Cardhu Distillery Visitor Centre.

2 Cardhu Distillery Visitor Centre

Cardhu is renowned among malt whisky connoisseurs for its silky flavours and has a fascinating hidden history, revealed at its visitor centre.

Return to Cardow village and turn right (southwest) on the B9102. Continue for 5km (3 miles) to Marypark. Turn right on the A95 main road and after 3km (2 miles) turn left on to the B9008. After 6.4km (4 miles), turn right to Glenlivet village and the distillery.

3 Glenlivet Distillery

One of the most famous Speyside whiskies, Glenlivet was one of the first to be exported worldwide. It is also one of the largest distilleries.

Continue south on the B9008 for 1.6km (1 mile), then turn left on the B9009 for 17km (10½ miles) to Dufftown. Turn left on the A941 from the town centre to the Glenfiddich Distillery, 500m (550 yards) from Dufftown.

4 Glenfiddich Distillery

Glenfiddich has been made here since 1887 and is the only Highland malt that is still distilled, aged and bottled all at its own distillery. The 'Original Tour' of the distillery is free.

Follow the A941 northwest for 5km (3 miles) to Craigellachie village.

5 Speyside Cooperage Visitor Centre

The cooperage's skilled coopers (barrel-makers) repair around 100,000 casks each year to supply the distilleries.

Follow the A941 for 5km (3 miles) to Rothes village and turn right to the Glen Grant Distillery.

6 Glen Grant Distillery and Garden

Founded in 1840, this distillery is surrounded by a lovely Victorian garden.

Continue north on the A941 for 16km (10 miles) to Elgin. The Glen Moray Distillery is just north of the town centre.

7 Glen Moray Distillery

Founded in 1897, this is another connoisseur's distillery.

The A96 west leads to Inverness.

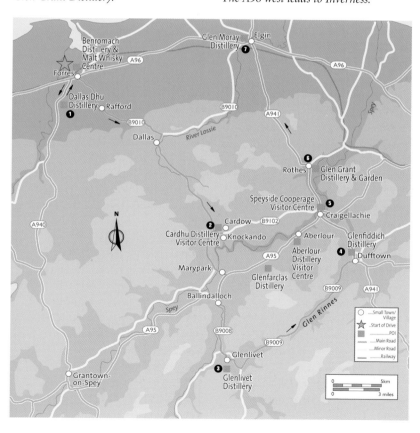

Highland Argyll

Argyll stretches from the northern shore of the Clyde to Fort William and the Great Glen. It is bordered to the east by mountains that separate it from Perthshire, and to the west by a wild and deeply indented coast dominated by deep sea lochs; the islands of the Inner Hebrides lie offshore. This was – and is – the territory of the Campbells, whose chiefs became the most powerful of the Highland magnates.

For the visitor, one of Argyll's main attractions is its accessibility. Loch Lomond, the western gateway to the Highlands, is less than an hour's drive away from Glasgow and its international airport, less than two hours from Edinburgh, and the A82 road, running north through the heart of Argyll, leads onwards to Inverness and the northern Highlands. Argyll also offers an excellent choice of activities, ranging from hillwalking and mountain biking to sea kayaking and scuba diving, and the coast is renowned for its seafood.

Fort William and Loch Linnhe

Fort William stands at the head of Loch Linnhe, the deep sea loch at the southern end of the Great Glen which stretches southwest to open into the Atlantic on the Firth of Lorn. It takes its name from the fortress built by Oliver Cromwell's right-hand man in Scotland, General Monk, and was the earliest of a chain of fortifications built along the line of the Great Glen to pacify the Highlands. It is also the southern end of the Caledonian Canal, the line of locks and canals designed by Thomas Telford and completed in 1882, linking Scotland's west coast with the Moray Firth in the northeast.

Today, it's a lively holiday town in summer, with plenty of places to stay, drink and eat, and a portfolio of activities and natural and man-made visitor attractions nearby.
103km (64 miles) southwest of Inverness.

Ben Nevis

Britain's highest mountain looms over Fort William and the coast, and its lower slopes are only 3km (2 miles) from town, at the head of Glen Nevis. Wild-looking but easily accessible, the pretty glen has been the backdrop for several films, including scenes from *Braveheart*, starring Mel Gibson, and *Rob Roy*, with Liam Neeson in the title role. At 1,344m (4,409ft), Ben Nevis is a challenging ascent, but it can be completed by any reasonably fit and experienced walker with the right equipment and in the right weather. Essentials include proper walking boots, warm clothes and wet-weather gear, plenty of food and drink, and a change of clothing. Inexperienced walkers should not attempt the climb without a guide, and only very experienced hillwalkers should attempt it in the winter months. Blizzard conditions are possible, and potentially dangerous, between October and May,

and wet weather and poor visibility are common at any time of year; weather can change rapidly and unpredictably.
3km (2 miles) east of Fort William.

Ben Nevis Distillery Visitor Centre
Tour of the distillery, audiovisual presentation on the making of whisky in the region, malt whisky tastings and a range of malt whiskies to buy and take away.
Lochy Bridge, 3.2km (2 miles) north of Fort William on the A82. Tel: (01397)

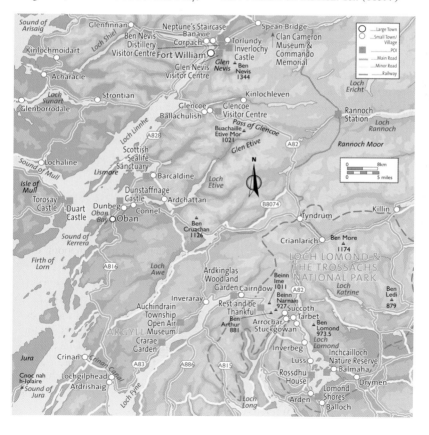

*700 200. www.bennevisdistillery.com.
Open: Jan–Jun & Sept–Dec Mon–Fri
9am–5pm; Easter–Sept Sat 10am–4pm;
Jul–Aug Mon–Fri 9am–6pm, Sun
noon–4pm. Admission charge.*

Clan Cameron Museum

The museum tells the story of Clan
Cameron's role (on the side of Bonnie
Prince Charlie) in the Jacobite rising of
1745–6, and of the Queen's Own
Cameron Highlanders, one of the
Highland Regiments raised to fight for
the British Crown after the final defeat
of the clans at Culloden.
*Achnacarry, Spean Bridge, 26km
(16 miles) northeast of Fort William on
the B8005. Tel: (01397) 712 480.
www.clan-cameron.org. Open: Apr–Jun
& Sept–mid-Oct daily 1.30–5pm;
Jul–Aug daily 11am–5pm. Closed: mid-
Oct–Mar. Admission charge.*

Commando Memorial

Britain's newly created special forces,
the Royal Marine Commandos, trained
in the wild countryside around Fort
William during World War II. This
statue, sculpted in 1952 by Scott
Sutherland, is their memorial.
*A82, 17.5km (11 miles) northeast of
Fort William.*

Glen Nevis Visitor Centre

Close to the foot of Ben Nevis, the
visitor centre is an essential stop for
those setting out to climb the hill.
It has a small exhibition on the history
of Ben Nevis and the glen, up-to-date
information on walking routes, weather
forecasts and a shop where you can
stock up on snacks and area maps.
*Glen Nevis, 3km (2 miles) east of
Fort William. Tel: (01397) 705 922.
Email: glen.nevis@highland.gov.uk.*

The access road to the Nevis Range Ski Centre, with Ben Nevis looming

*Open: Apr–Oct daily 10am–5pm.
Closed: Nov–Mar. Free admission.*

Inverlochy Castle
This remarkably intact square keep
with a round tower at each corner was
built in the 13th century by the Comyn
family, rivals of Robert the Bruce.
*3km (2 miles) northeast of Fort William.
Tel: (01667) 460 232. www.historic-
scotland.gov.uk. Open: times vary – see
website or call. Admission charge.*

Nevis Range
In winter, the only mountain gondola
in the UK takes skiers and
snowboarders to 655.3m (2,150ft) on
the face of Aonach Mor. In summer
(mid-May to mid-September), you can
take the gondola to the summit and
return by one of several mountain-bike
tracks. There are superb views of
nearby Ben Nevis from the top of
Aonach Mor.
*Torlundy, northeast of Fort William.
Tel: (01397) 705 825. www.nevisrange.
co.uk. Open: mid-Dec–mid-Nov daily,
dawn until dusk. Closed: mid-Nov–mid-
Dec. Admission charge.*

Treasures of the Earth
A huge collection of crystals and
precious and semi-precious stones is
displayed in a series of artificial caves,
grottoes and gemstone mines.
*Corpach, north of Fort William.
Tel: (01397) 772 283. Open: May–Sept
daily 9.30am–7pm; Oct–Apr daily
10am–5pm. Admission charge.*

West Highland Museum
This museum has an excellent but
slightly old-fashioned collection of
tartan, portraits of clansmen and
chieftains, mementos of Bonnie Prince
Charlie, Highland silver and glassware,
and a weaponry collection including
dirks, Doune pistols and broadswords
and the terrifying Lochaber axe.
*Cameron Square, Fort William.
Tel: (01397) 702 169.
www.westhighlandmuseum.org.uk.
Open: Jun–Sept Mon–Sat 10am–5pm,
Sun (Jul–Aug) 10am–4pm; Oct–May
Mon–Sat 10am–4pm. Admission charge.*

Glencoe
Travelling through Glencoe is like
stepping into a romantic Highland
landscape painted by Landseer or one
of his imitators. The glen is a study in
purple heather, grey granite, russet
bracken and sparkling water, marked by
sweeping cloud-shadows. It is also the
setting of one of the most infamous
episodes in the violent history of the
Highlands: the Massacre of Glencoe.
In 1692, a party of Campbell soldiers,
acting on the orders of Dalrymple, the
master of the Stair estate and King
William's leading Scots henchman,
turned on their hosts, the MacDonalds
of Glencoe, slaughtering men, women
and children and driving the survivors
into the snow to freeze or starve. The
MacDonalds' crime was that their chief
had been late in taking the oath of
allegiance to the new king; Stair
intended to set a bloody example to

View up Glencoe past Loch Achtriochtan

other recalcitrant clans, and the Campbells were keen as ever to curry favour with the new government.

The A82 crosses through the Pass of Glencoe between Crianlarich and Fort William, and through the villages of **Ballachulish** and Glencoe, near the foot of the glen.

Ballachulish Visitor Centre, Ballachulish, 27km (17 miles) south of Fort William. Tel: (01855) 811 866. www.glencoetourism.com. Open: Jun–Aug daily 9am–6pm; Sept–May Mon–Sat 9am–5pm, Sun 10am–5pm.

Glencoe and North Lorn Folk Museum

This small museum in a group of traditional heather-thatched buildings offers a peek into Highland traditions and country life and the wildlife and natural history of the Glencoe area.

Glencoe village, A82, 34km (21 miles) south of Fort William. Tel: (01855) 811 664. Open: Apr–Oct Mon–Sat 10am–5.30pm. Closed: Nov–Mar & Sun. Admission charge for adults.

Glencoe Visitor Centre

The tragic history, spectacular landscapes and wildlife of one of Scotland's most beautiful glens are highlighted in the National Trust for Scotland's Glencoe Visitor Centre and an outstanding exhibition, *Living on the Edge*. The centre also offers guided walks in Glencoe, including a walk to Signal Rock, where the signal is said to have been given in 1692 for King William's Campbell redcoats to begin the notorious massacre.

Near Ballachulish, A82, 27km (17 miles) south of Fort William. Tel: (01855) 811

307. www.glencoe-nts.org.uk. Open: end Mar–Aug daily 9.30am–5.30pm; Sept–Oct daily 10am–5pm; Nov–end Mar Thur–Sun 10am–4pm. Admission charge.

Inveraray

On the north shore of Loch Fyne, Inveraray is a tidy historic town which has been the seat of the dukes of Argyll, the senior branch of the Campbell clan, since the early 15th century, when they moved south from their previous home on Loch Awe to this more accessible location (Loch Awe is landlocked, while Loch Fyne opens on to the Firth of Clyde and the Irish Sea). The town owes its major landmark, Inveraray Castle, as well as many of its public buildings, to the dukes of Argyll.

32km (20 miles) west of Tarbet on the A83.

Duke's Tower

Looming over Inveraray town centre, this granite tower houses the second-heaviest ten-bell carillon in the world. A stairway leads to a viewing gallery from which you can watch the bell-ringers at work, and from which there are excellent views of Inveraray and its surroundings. If the bells are not ringing, you can listen to a recording of their sound.

The Avenue, Inveraray. Open: May–Sept daily 10am–1pm & 2–5pm. Closed: Oct–Apr. Admission charge.

Inveraray sits on the shores of Loch Fyne

Inveraray Castle

The first Campbell castle here was a workmanlike, defensive keep built in the 15th century, when the Campbell chiefs first made Inveraray their seat. The Campbells had their enemies, and felt safer behind fortifications. The present castle – although it looks romantically medieval, with turrets and battlements – dates from the second half of the 18th century, when the pacification of the Highlands allowed the Campbells to dispense with their ancient defences and build a more comfortable home. The architects were Robert Mylne and Roger Morris. You can trace the complex family tree of the Campbells in the Clan Room and admire a famous collection of medieval arms and armour, fine furniture, French tapestries, paintings and prints.

Inveraray, A83, 1km (²/₃ mile) north of the town centre. Tel: (01499) 202 203. www.inveraray-castle.com. Open: Apr–Oct daily 10am–5.45pm. Tours: 11am & 2pm. Last admission 5pm. Closed: Nov–Mar. Admission charge.

Across the waters of Aray to Inveraray Castle

The members of the jury at Inveraray Jail

Inveraray Jail

Inveraray's former jailhouse and courtroom are brought to life by actor-guides playing the roles of warders and prisoners in the 19th century. Punishments such as the whipping table and the crank are contrasted with the relatively enlightened regime in modern Scottish jails in a new exhibition, *In Prison Today*. The whole experience is guaranteed to make the average visitor resolve to stay on the right side of the law.
Church Square, Inveraray.
Tel: (01499) 302 381.
www.inverarayjail.co.uk. Open: Apr–Oct daily 9.30am–6pm; Nov–Mar daily 10am–5pm. Last admission one hour before closing. Admission charge.

Inveraray Maritime Museum

Documentary film footage, charts and documents, prints and photographs and an array of maritime paraphernalia are exhibited aboard the veteran vessel *Arctic Penguin*, built in 1911. Lifelike figures in the hold give you some idea of just how miserable life was aboard the emigrant ships that carried Highland folk into exile in Canada and America at the time of the Clearances.
The Pier, Inveraray. Tel: (01499) 302 213. www.inveraraypier.com. Open: daily 10am–6pm. Admission charge.

Walk: Around Inveraray

Inveraray is one of the prettiest small towns in the Highlands; its carefully planned streets are lined with sturdy white-painted houses and gracious public buildings. Most of the town dates from the second half of the 18th century, when the dukes of Argyll created a new settlement to rehouse their tenants while at the same time building a grand new castle for themselves.

Allow 4 hours to complete this walk.

Start at Inveraray Castle.

1 Inveraray Castle

The present Inveraray Castle was begun in 1746 but was not completed until around 1789. It is perhaps the finest castle in the Highlands (outdoing even Balmoral) and is still the home of the 13th Duke of Argyll.

Leave the castle grounds, turn right on to the A83 main road, and walk about 100m (110 yards) south to the beginning of Front Street. About 100m (110 yards) down the street, turn right through an elegant, three-arched arcade into The Avenue. Follow this broad, tree-lined street for 250m (275 yards) to the town's most prominent landmark, which cannot be missed.

2 Duke's Tower

The granite bell tower, which stands a little to the south of All Saints' Church, has the heaviest ten-bell peal in Scotland and was commissioned following World War I by the tenth

Duke of Argyll as a memorial to the Campbell soldiers killed in that conflict. Climb the tower to the viewing gallery for great views of Inveraray.

Cross The Avenue and walk east for 100m (110 yards) to the corner of Main Street and Church Square.

3 Inveraray Church

Inveraray's elegant neoclassical church, designed by Robert Mylne, was once two churches in one, with one part for the local Gaelic-speaking congregation and the other half serving the English-speaking community. With the decline of Gaelic, the northern half of the church is now the church hall.

Cross to the east side of the square to Inveraray Jail and Courthouse.

4 Inveraray Jail and Courthouse

The jail ceased to be used as a place of incarceration in the 1930s, and its cell blocks and courtroom are now an entertaining and educational museum, where actor-guides bring it to life.

From the square, walk north for 100m (110 yards) along Main Street to the corner of Front Street. Immediately in front of you is a stone cross.

5 Inveraray Cross

Decorated with complex intertwining patterns, the cross is a fine example of the medieval Iona School of Celtic carving.

Turn right, walk 50m (55 yards) along the lochside, then turn left on to the pier. The vintage vessel Arctic Penguin,

with its three masts, is moored on the north side.

6 Inveraray Maritime Museum

The *Arctic Penguin*, one of the last of the steel-hulled sailing ships, was built in Dublin in 1911. On board are maritime paraphernalia and a small exhibition focusing on 19th-century emigration from the Highlands.

Return to the foot of the pier and walk the length of Front Street, to return to the castle grounds.

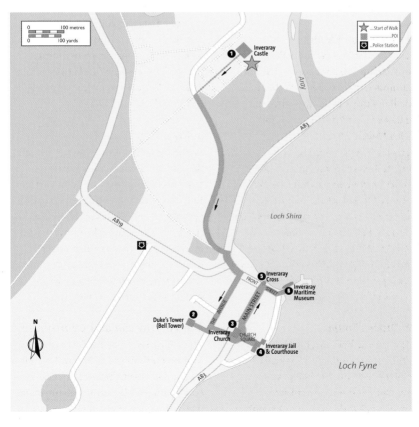

Loch Fyne

This narrow, crooked sea loch curves southwest from Inveraray for some 50km (30 miles) before reaching the Sound of Bute and the Firth of Clyde. The A83 runs along the north shore of Loch Fyne, then turns north through Lochgilphead and on to Oban on the west coast of Argyll.

Ardkinglas Woodland Garden

Red squirrels scamper among the huge fir and pine trees in Scotland's most spectacular collection of mighty conifers; the largest tree is a silver fir with a circumference of almost 10m (33ft). When in full flower in spring and early summer, the rhododendron gardens are dazzlingly colourful.
Ardkinglas Estate, Cairndow, on the A83, 13km (8 miles) northeast of Inveraray. Tel: (01499) 600 261.

The pier at Inversnaid on the eastern shore of Loch Lomond

www.ardkinglas.com. Open: daily, dawn until dusk. Admission charge.

Auchindrain Township Open Air Museum

This unique 'township' or communally tenanted farming village has changed little over centuries and gives a glimpse of life in a traditional Highland village. It is the only medieval township to have survived on its original site, and its farmlands, homes and farm buildings have been preserved as they were in the late 19th century. A new café-restaurant is scheduled to open here in 2011.
North shore of Loch Fyne on the A83, 10km (6 miles) southwest of Inveraray. Tel: (01499) 500 235. www.auchindrain-museum.org.uk. Open: Apr–Sept daily 10am–5pm. Closed: Oct–Mar. Admission charge.

Crarae Garden

This lovely wooded glen is full of cascades and streams that eventually flow into Loch Fyne, and is lushly planted with shrubs and trees from the temperate zones of every continent.
North shore of Loch Fyne on the A83, 16km (10 miles) southwest of Inveraray. Tel: (01546) 603 210. www.nts.org.uk. Open: daily, 9.30am until dusk. Visitor centre open: Apr–Oct Thur–Mon 10am–5pm. Admission charge.

Crinan Canal

The Crinan Canal with its 15 locks was built between 1793 and 1801 to connect Ardrishaig, just south of Lochgilphead on Loch Fyne, with Crinan on the Sound of Jura, thus allowing vessels to reach the Atlantic Ocean without making the long voyage round the Mull of Kintyre. The 14.5km (9-mile) canal is now used only by yachts and cruisers, but the towpath is a great place for an undemanding stroll, and at the Crinan end there are splendid views westwards over the Sound to Jura and Mull.

Canal Office: Pier Square, Ardrishaig. Tel: (01546) 603 210. www.scottishcanals.co.uk. Open: daily 8.30am–5pm.

Loch Lomond

Surrounded by wooded hillsides and dotted with small, pretty islands, Loch Lomond is the largest body of fresh water in Britain and rivals Loch Ness as Scotland's best-known loch, thanks to Robert Burns's ballad 'The Bonnie Banks of Loch Lomond' – as well as the TV series *Take the High Road*, whose title was taken from the song's refrain.

The southern end of the loch is only a short drive from the outskirts of Glasgow and is a popular weekend getaway for city-dwellers, some of whom keep yachts and motor-cruisers on its marina. By contrast, the northern end of the loch stretches deep into wilder Highland landscapes. Loch Lomond and its numerous islands form part of the Loch Lomond and the Trossachs National Park, which stretches northwest to include the hills of the Trossachs, once the haunt of the outlawed Rob Roy MacGregor. The park also encloses the peaks of Ben Lomond (973.5m/3,194ft), one of Scotland's most impressive mountains, on the northeast side of the loch, Ben More (1,174m/3,853ft) and Ben Ledi (879m/2,885ft), as well as pretty Loch Katrine, in the very centre of the park.

Access to Ben Lomond from the B837 road, 17.5km (11 miles) north of Drymen village. Tel: (01360) 870 224.

Looking north along the banks of Loch Lomond

Rob Roy: hero or villain?

Like Robin Hood, Ned Kelly or Jesse James, Rob Roy MacGregor has been immortalised in print and on film as a wronged and romantic outlaw-hero – first as the eponymous hero in Sir Walter Scott's novel, and more recently by Hollywood with Liam Neeson in the title role. As always, the truth behind the legend is a little less glamorous.

Living in the glens of the Trossachs, within easy raiding distance of prosperous Lowland farming country, the MacGregor clan often yielded to the temptation to lift a few head of cattle. They were also in a near-permanent state of feud with their powerful neighbours, the Campbells, and indeed with most of the other neighbouring clans. Unlike the canny Campbells, the MacGregors had the knack of picking the losing side in many of the conflicts that wracked the Highlands, and in 1603, after a raid on the lands of the Colquhouns of Rossdhu and a pitched battle between Colquhouns and MacGregors at Glen Fruin, their name was proscribed by the Crown, their chief hanged in Edinburgh, and their lands forfeited.

Rob Roy was born 69 years after these events, the son of Donald Glas MacGregor, one of the outlawed clan's senior men, and Margaret

Rob Roy's grave in front of Balquhidder Old Kirk

The Rob Roy and Trossachs Visitor Centre at Callander

Campbell. By Highland standards he was well educated, speaking and writing English as well as his native Gaelic, and was also a noted swordsman. Like the later outlaws of the American West, he supplemented a little farming on the banks of Loch Lomond with a more lucrative trade in cattle droving, cattle stealing, and extorting protection money from his less warlike neighbours. Typically, the MacGregors chose to support the deposed King James VII and II against the Protestant William of Orange, and Rob Roy and his father both served with Claverhouse's victorious Highland army at Killiecrankie in 1689. After the armistice that followed the final Williamite victory in 1691, he went almost legitimate, as a member of the Lennox Watch – a militia set up to deter cattle thieves – and as a cattle dealer. At first, he prospered, selling Scottish cattle in England at a handsome profit, but in 1712 he borrowed £1,000 from the Duke of Montrose to finance a cattle deal that went wrong when one of his men absconded with the money. Montrose had him declared a thief and a bankrupt, and the soldiers that he sent to seize Rob Roy's lands also (according to the legend) raped his wife. Taking to the hills, Rob Roy eventually gained the protection of the Earl of Breadalbane – a political enemy of Montrose's – who granted him land in Glen Dochart, and Rob Roy returned to 'protecting' cattle and raiding Montrose's own herds in a personal feud.

In 1715, he brought a MacGregor faction out to campaign for the 'Old Pretender'. With the failure of that rising, he was amnestied, but went back to harassing Montrose. He was twice captured, but escaped each time. By 1720, when Rob Roy settled down at Balquhidder, Montrose had given up hunting him, and the rest of his life was surprisingly tranquil. He died in 1734, at the age of 63 – a ripe old age for a Highland outlaw and cattle thief.

Balloch

Balloch, on the south shore of Loch Lomond, is the main gateway to the loch and a base for watersports, fishing and other activities.

Cruises around Loch Lomond and its islands operate from Balloch all year round.

Sweeney's Cruises, Riverside, Balloch. Tel: (01389) 752 376 for timetables. www.sweeney.uk.com

Inchcailloch Nature Reserve

Inchcailloch, on the east side of Loch Lomond, is the most accessible island in the loch. The nature reserve protects ancient and unique oak woodland and is a refuge for a number of wild animal species, including roe deer. Camping is permitted (at the official site) and there is a barbecue and picnic area and a beach, as well as some 3km (2 miles) of marked walking trails.

Inchcailloch, Loch Lomond, opposite Balmaha; ferry from McFarlane's boatyard, Balmaha. Tel: (01786) 450 362. www.lochlomond-trossachs.org

Lomond Shores

This enormous modern shopping and leisure mall just northwest of Balloch at the south end of the loch is incongruous amid the natural beauty of Loch Lomond, but does provide a plethora of all-weather attractions and activities, a children's play area, lots of places to eat and drink and even its own beach and picnic areas. A widescreen film presentation, *Legend of Loch Lomond*, romanticises the history of the region, but the new Seaquarium attraction with its huge tanks full of marine and freshwater creatures is well worth visiting. Moored a few hundred

Traditional boats for hire at McFarlane's boatyard in Balmaha

The main street in Luss, on the west coast of Loch Lomond

yards east of Lomond Shores is the largest inland vessel ever built in Britain, the *Maid of the Loch*. Launched in 1953 and mothballed in 1989, this vintage paddle steamer is being restored and may one day sail on the loch again. The steamer houses a restaurant, café and bar and a souvenir shop.

Lomond Shores, 1km (²/₃ mile) northwest of Balloch village centre.
Tel: (01389) 751 035.
www.lochlomondshores.com. Open: daily 9am–7pm. Lomond Shores mall free; admission charge for attractions.
Maid of the Loch *paddle steamer tel: (01389) 711 865.*
www.maidoftheloch.com. Open: Easter–Oct daily 11am–4pm; winter Sat–Sun 11am–4pm. Admission charge.

Luss

Luss is a postcard-pretty 'model village' of whitewashed cottages on the west shore of the loch, built during the late 18th century by the laird of Rossdhu, the biggest landowner in these parts, to provide new and improved housing for his tenants.

A82, 14km (8²/₃ miles) north of Balloch.

Tarbet

Tarbet, on the west shore of the loch, is the departure point for **cruises** on the narrow northern section of Loch Lomond, with splendid views of Ben Lomond on the opposite shore. From here, you can carry on north on the A82 towards Fort William or head west on the A83 to Inveraray, Loch Fyne and Oban.

Cruise Loch Lomond, The Boatyard, Tarbet. West shore of Loch Lomond on the A82, 16km (10 miles) north of Balloch. Tel: (01301) 702 356.
www.cruiselochlomond.co.uk.
Departures all year daily – call for tailored itineraries or see website for timings of scheduled cruises.

Drive: Loch Lomond to Loch Fyne

This 65km (40-mile) drive from Balloch to Inveraray takes you through some of the prettiest scenery in Scotland and is a perfect introduction to the beautiful loch, sea and mountain landscapes of the Highlands. Beginning on the outskirts of Glasgow, the route quickly plunges into wild countryside. This is really a drive for a summer's day.

Allow 4 hours with stops.

1 Balloch

An unassuming small tourist town at the southernmost point of Loch Lomond, Balloch is the main gateway to the loch and a base for watersports, fishing and other activities.

The south shore is the widest stretch of Loch Lomond and is dotted with an archipelago of small, wooded islands. The southernmost, Inchmurrin, lies a little way north of Arden village.
Leaving Balloch, turn right on the A82. Head north, keeping the loch on your right. About 8km (5 miles) after leaving Balloch, pass a sign on your right to Rossdhu House.

2 Rossdhu House

The former home of the Colquhoun clan chiefs, this grand Georgian building surrounded by rhododendron gardens is now the clubhouse of the Loch Lomond Golf Club.
Members and guests only. www.lochlomond.com. Approximately 6km (3½ miles) north of Rossdhu is Luss.

3 Luss

This quaintly pretty village, with its whitewashed houses, was built by a benevolent laird of Rossdhu as a model village to provide better housing than the traditional turf-walled 'black houses' of the Highlands.
Continue north on the A82, passing through Inverbeg and Stuckgowan, for just over 13km (8 miles) to Tarbet.

4 Tarbet

As you head north from Luss, the loch narrows and becomes more steep sided. Opposite Tarbet, Ben Lomond looms massively over the calm water. Tarbet is the departure point for cruises on this narrow northern part of the loch.
At Tarbet, turn left (west) on the A83 through Arrochar at the head of Loch Long. The road skirts the head of the loch, passes through the small village of Succoth, then turns southwest, and not long after turns sharply northwest, away from the loch.

5 Glen Croe

The road now passes through a narrow and pretty glen, Glen Croe, and climbs steeply. Looming on your right are the peaks of Ben Arthur, Beinn Narnain and Beinn Ime. After about 8km (5 miles) you reach the saddle of the pass, which is appropriately named Rest and be Thankful.

Continue down Glen Kinglas on the A83 for 8km (5 miles), bypassing Ardkinglas village, to Cairndow and Ardkinglas Woodland Garden.

6 Ardkinglas Woodland Garden

Ardkinglas has one of the finest collections of conifer trees in Britain.
Ardkinglas Estate, Cairndow. Tel: (01499) 600 261. www.ardkinglas.com. Open: daily, dawn until dusk. Admission charge.
Follow the A83 for 16km (10 miles) before arriving at Inveraray.

7 Inveraray

This town owes its existence to the dukes of Argyll, who built a castle (*see p72*).

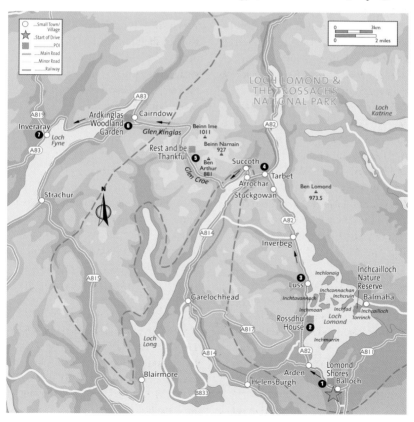

Oban

Oban is a lively fishing harbour and holiday town on the west coast, facing on to Oban Bay and the Sound of Kerrera. Sheltered from the open waters of the Firth of Lorn by the small island of Kerrera, and with outlets to the sea from the north and south, it is to this excellent natural anchorage that Oban owes its long history as a seaport, stretching back more than a thousand years to the days of the Vikings and the lords of the Isles. Oban has more than its fair share of places to stay, pubs and restaurants, and is an excellent base for exploring the Argyll coast. With ferries to several islands – including Mull, Lismore and Colonsay – it is a handy getaway from which to escape to the Inner Hebrides, and it is also a popular watersports base, offering sailing, scuba diving, windsurfing and marine wildlife cruises. Loch Etive, a long and narrow sea loch more than 24km (15 miles) in length, meets the Firth of Lorn about 5km (3 miles) north of Oban.
A85/A828, 48km (30 miles) south of Fort William.

Ardchattan Gardens and Priory

Overlooking Loch Etive, the 1.6 hectares (4 acres) of landscaped lawns, borders and rockeries surround the ruins of an ancient chapel.
Ardchattan, 8km (5 miles) northeast of Connel, on the north side of Loch Etive. Tel: (01796) 481 355. www.gardens-of-argyll.co.uk. Open: Apr–Oct daily 9am–5pm. Closed: Nov–Mar. Admission charge.

A ferry departing the harbour at Oban

The graveyard at Ardchattan Priory, a 13th-century ruin

Dunstaffnage Castle

Massive walls defend the ruins of this mighty stronghold of the MacDougalls on its crag beside the Firth of Lorn. Built in the second half of the 13th century, the seemingly impregnable castle was nevertheless taken by Robert the Bruce in 1309. Flora MacDonald, the Highland noblewoman who helped Charles Edward Stuart flee to Skye and then to France after his defeat at Culloden, was briefly imprisoned here in 1746.

Dunbeg, off the A85, 4.8km (3 miles) north of Oban. Tel: (01631) 562 465. www.historic-scotland.gov.uk. Open: Apr–Sept daily 9.30am–5.30pm; Oct daily 9.30am–4.30pm; Nov–Mar Sat–Wed 9.30am–4.30pm. Admission charge.

Oban Distillery Visitor Centre

The visitor centre has an exhibition showing something of Oban's history and more about the history of distilling in the area. There are guided tours of the distillery, an audiovisual show and a shop selling souvenirs and single malt whiskies.

Stafford Street, Oban. Tel: (01631) 572 004. www.discovering-distilleries.com. Open: Feb & Dec Mon–Fri 12.30–4pm; Mar–Easter & Nov Mon–Fri 10am–5pm; Easter–Jun & Oct Mon–Sat 9.30am–5pm; Jul–Sept Mon–Fri 9.30am–7.30pm, Sat–Sun 9.30am–5pm. Closed: Jan.

Scottish Sealife Sanctuary

Seals and otters that have been found sick or injured are nursed back to health here before being released back into the wild, and seabirds and other local sea creatures can also be seen. This is one of Scotland's leading marine conservation centres.

Barcaldine, by Oban. Tel: (01631) 720 386. www.sealsanctuary.co.uk. Open: daily 10am–5pm. Admission charge.

A chequered history: Highland dress

The tartan kilt is recognised around the world as the symbol of Scotland and the Highlands.

Ironically, the kilt as it is known today and the many different clan and regimental tartans are quite recent inventions.

In the golden age before the final conquest by the Hanoverian regime, the typical dress of the Highland

A piper in full Highland dress

clansman was the plaid. This was a great length of woollen cloth, dyed with natural pigments that matched the colours of the Highland landscape, which was excellent camouflage for raiders or fugitives. The wearer used it as a blanket at night and literally rolled himself into his plaid in the morning, binding it with belts and bandoliers that held his weapons and other valuables. The sporran, a leather pouch on a waist belt, held his few smaller possessions. His only other garment was a long linen shirt, often dyed saffron yellow. To foreign eyes, the Highlander must have appeared a shaggy and uncivilised sight.

After the brutal quelling of the 1745 Jacobite rising, tartan and the plaid – along with other symbols of the old clan way of life, such as pipe music – were banned. By the early 19th century, however, this prohibition had been lifted. Highland Regiments, each with its own distinctive tartan, had joined the British Army. By the 1820s, when King George IV's visit to Scotland sparked a new fascination with the

Kilts are mainly worn at formal occasions and celebrations

'romantic' Highlands, tartan and the kilt were reborn. The untidy plaid mutated into the neatly pleated kilt (or *philibeg*, to give it its Gaelic name) and acquired a suite of new accoutrements. An entire industry grew up, inventing and weaving new tartans for each clan, as well as for those with Lowland surnames, too. Today, there is even a Singh tartan, created in honour of Scotland's first Sikh peer.

Only a few people wear the kilt as everyday wear, but the full outfit comes out for weddings and other formal occasions. Since devolution, it has become fashionable party wear, and kilts can now be found not only in traditional tartans but in bright colours, polka dots, stars and stripes and even black leather. The sporran, traditionally made from sealskin, is now more often made from leather or fur from non-threatened animals or from artificial materials.

The full formal Highland outfit of kilt, short black silver-buttoned jacket, sporran, knee-length woollen hose, dress shoes and short *sgian dubh* dagger with an amethyst or tourmaline set in its pommel can cost up to £900, but you can find cheap and cheerful kilts and accessories in high-street shops for as little as £80. And one thing has not changed: as any true Highlander will tell you, nothing is worn under the kilt…

Inverness and around

Inverness is Scotland's newest city, awarded the status in 2001. Although a castle stood here as early as the 12th century, the 'Capital of the Highlands' really came into its own only in the 18th and 19th centuries. This region is home to Culloden Moor, where Charles Edward Stuart's Jacobite clansmen made their last stand against the Duke of Cumberland's redcoats on 16 April 1746, and the most famous of Scottish lakes, Loch Ness.

Deep, dark and mysterious, Loch Ness continues to attract hundreds of thousands of visitors hoping for a glimpse of the legendary monster – despite the lack of any shred of evidence that it exists. This part of the Highlands can be visited at any time of year, but the best time to go is between June and September. Winter landscapes can be spectacular, with snow-capped peaks all around Inverness as late as May. However, the region gets little more than six hours of daylight in midwinter, and cold, wet weather can be expected from October to April.

Beauly

The small town of Beauly, near Inverness, lies at the head of the lovely Beauly Firth, where dolphins and seals may sometimes be seen. It is surrounded by the most spectacular mountain scenery.
19km (12 miles) west of Inverness on the A9.

Beauly Priory Visitor Centre

Beauly Priory, founded by the Valliscaulian order around 1230, was partly rebuilt in the 1530s. It now lies in ruins but many of its beautiful original features can still be seen.
The Square, Beauly. Tel: (01463) 783 444. www.historic-scotland.gov.uk. Open: daily 10am–4pm. Admission charge.

Culloden

Culloden is the site of one of the most famous decisive battles in British history and is easily visited from Inverness on an escorted tour or by using public transport. Near the battlefield is one of Scotland's most important prehistoric sites.
8km (5 miles) east of Inverness on the B9006.

Clava Cairns

Rings of standing stones surround two unimaginably ancient chambered cairns and a 'ring cairn' dating from the late Neolithic era or the early Bronze

Age, making them among the oldest buildings in Britain.

Clava, 1.6km (1 mile) east of Culloden off the B9006. Tel: (01667) 460 232. www.historic-scotland.gov.uk. Open: daily, dawn until dusk.

Culloden Battlefield Visitor Centre

The battle that took place at Culloden Moor on 16 April 1746 finally crushed the Stuart dynasty's hopes of reclaiming the British throne. It also spelt the beginning of the end of the clan system and the traditional Highland way of life. Outnumbered and outgunned by the Duke of Cumberland's redcoats, Bonnie Prince Charlie's army was destroyed in less than an hour. Around the battlefield, memorials and clan graves mark where the Jacobite warriors fell, and the moor has been returned to the state it was in on the day of the battle, with reconstructed dykes (dry stone walls) and a small

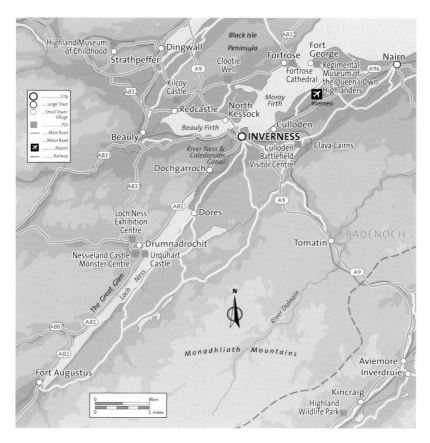

stone cottage around which the fighting raged. The visitor centre has an outstanding new collection of original weapons and documents and an array of authentic replica Highland weapons made in the traditional manner by modern master craftsmen. The visitor centre also explodes some of the myths surrounding Culloden and the '45 rising and explains that it was not a simple matter of Scots against English – there were Highland and Lowland Scots on both sides at Culloden.

Culloden Moor, Inverness. Tel: (01463) 790 607. www.nts.org.uk. Battlefield open: daily, dawn until dusk.
Visitor Centre, Culloden, open: Apr–Oct daily 9am–6pm; Nov–Mar daily 10am–4pm. Free admission.

Fort George

Work on this huge and impressive fortification began after the Battle of Culloden and was completed in 1769. With about 1km (²/₃ mile) of walls and strategically sited on a headland which juts into the Moray Firth, Fort George is the largest artillery fortress in Britain and was intended to prevent any further attempts by the French to land troops to support yet another Jacobite rebellion. In fact, the French made no such attempt after Culloden, and Fort George's guns were never fired in anger. The fort is still a military garrison, and contains the **Regimental Museum of the Queen's Own Highlanders**. Visitors can see the old barrack rooms, and there is an excellent collection of 18th-century weaponry.

Inverness has a compact city centre

The Greig Street footbridge across the River Ness, an Inverness icon

18km (11 miles) northeast of Inverness, off the A96. Tel: (01667) 460 232. www.historic-scotland.gov.uk. Open: Apr–Sept daily 9.30am–6.30pm; Oct–Mar daily 9.30am–5.30pm. Admission charge.

Inverness

Inverness, the 'capital of the Highlands', straddles the River Ness between the northeast end of Loch Ness and the Moray Firth, a wide inlet that opens into the North Sea. This lively small city has a thriving tourism industry and plenty of hotels and places to eat and drink, but there are few outstanding visitor attractions within the city itself. A dramatic-looking 18th-century castle, on the north bank of the River Ness, dominates the city centre and houses the region's court, council offices and police headquarters.

Inverness Tourist Office: Castle Wynd/ Bridge Street. Tel: (01463) 234 353. www.visithighlands.com. Open: late Mar– late May & mid-Sept–Dec Mon–Sat 9am–5pm, Sun 10am–4pm; late May– late Jun & early–mid-Sept Mon–Sat 9am–6pm, Sun 9am–4pm; late Jun–Aug Mon–Sat 9am–6pm, Sun 9.30am–5pm. Closed: Jan–late Mar.

Inverness Cathedral

Overlooking the river, Inverness Cathedral (the Cathedral Church of St Andrew) is a relatively modern building, constructed in 1866–9. The Gothic building has twin towers with a carillon of ten bells and has attractive stained-glass windows.

11 Kenneth Street, Inverness. Tel: (01463) 225 553. www.invernesscathedral.co.uk. Open: daily 7.30am–6pm. Free admission.

Inverness Museum and Art Gallery

This small museum has a collection of fine Highland silver, traditional musical instruments, Highland dress and traditional weapons. It also has displays on natural history and wildlife.

Castle Wynd, Inverness. Tel: (01463) 237 114. www.inverness.highland.museum. Open: Mon–Sat 10am–5pm. Closed: Sun. Free admission.

Bonnie Prince Charlie and the Jacobite cause

Charles Edward Stuart, also known as 'Bonnie Prince Charlie' and the 'Young Pretender', was born in France, son of the exiled 'Old Pretender', and grandson of James II and VII, the last Stuart king of Scotland and England; the Jacobites, as Stuart partisans were known, took their name from 'Jacobus', the Latin version of 'James'.

He was raised in France and Italy, and spent less than a year of his life in Scotland. In the summer of 1745, he landed at Knoydart on the west coast of Scotland, with a handful of followers, to raise the clans in revolt against the Hanoverian King George II and reclaim the throne.

Despite what Highland patriots may tell you, Charles Edward was in no way fighting for a free Scotland. He wanted the British crown, and had the Jacobite cause been successful he would have reimposed an intolerant, autocratic Catholic monarchy and turned Britain into a satellite of France. Nor was the battle of '46 simply a matter of Scots versus English: there were Lowland Scots in Charles's army (along with French and

Irish mercenaries), and Highlanders on the government side.

At first, the Jacobites seemed destined for glory. Edinburgh opened its gates to Charles after his Highlanders routed Sir John Cope's government troops at Prestonpans, and the Jacobites marched into England as far as Derby. But the French reinforcements never turned up, and the Jacobites fell back into the Highlands, where on 16 April 1746 they were crushed by the Duke of Cumberland's redcoats in less than an hour's fighting. Some 1,250 Highlanders were killed, for the loss of just 50 Hanoverian troops. Hundreds more, including women and children, were murdered in cold blood, on the orders of the Duke of Cumberland.

After the battle, Charles fled the field before the battle was even over, earning him the scorn of at least one of his own generals. 'There you go for a damned cowardly Italian,' said Lord Elcho. After Culloden, Charles skulked through the Highlands, sheltered by a handful of loyalists. Romantics claim that even with a

Monument commemorating the 1745 rising when the Jacobites raised the standard of Bonnie Prince Charlie, Loch Shiel

price of £30,000 on his head, no Highlander would betray him to the redcoats. In fact, there were plenty who would have been happy to do so. Luckily for Charles, though, none of them knew where he was. Not long after Culloden, he slipped across to the Isle of Skye, dressed as a maid, in the entourage of Flora MacDonald, a clan chief's daughter. From there, he escaped to France, where he became a sad, brandy-sodden hanger-on at the court of Louis XV. Charles eventually returned to Italy, where he died in 1788.

Tour: Inverness to Kyle of Lochalsh by train

Britain's most dramatic rail journey winds its way from Inverness to Kyle of Lochalsh, traversing rolling moorland, haunted glens and heather-covered mountains. This is the heartland of the Highland clans, and is dotted with their castles.

Allow 4 hours.

Start in Inverness.

1 Inverness

Completed in 1870, the line is a living testament to the steam-age engineering skills of the Victorian railway engineers and navvies who blasted their way through tonnes of solid rock to link the east and west coasts. There are up to three departures daily from Inverness in high season. For details, contact **First ScotRail** (*Tel: (0845) 22 55 121. www.firstgroup.com*). Be warned that accommodation in the village of Kyle of Lochalsh is very limited and must be booked in advance.

Leaving Inverness, the train crosses the River Ness and the easternmost section of the Caledonian Canal, the chain of locks and canals that connects the lochs of the Great Glen. Within 15 minutes the train reaches Beauly.

2 Beauly Firth

The line runs along the south shore of the Beauly Firth, and it is worth keeping a keen eye out for seals and dolphins, as these waters shelter large populations of both. Look out, too, for the stone towers of Redcastle and Kilcoy Castle, centuries-old keeps of the Mackenzies, and – after crossing the River Beauly (about 25 minutes after leaving Inverness) – the 800-year-old Beauly Priory.

The flat moorland of Easter Ross can seem an anticlimax, but after the market town of Dingwall the line swings westwards and into increasingly dramatic scenery.

3 Glen Carron

The summit of 400m (1,312ft) Sgurr a' Mhuilinn overlooks the line before it crosses the Drumalbain watershed, Glen Carron, and the thick, ancient woodland of Achnashellach Forest, where with luck you may glimpse herds of deer.

After about 30 minutes, the line reaches the waters of Loch Carron, Loch Kishorn and the deeply indented Atlantic coastline.

4 Loch Kishorn

Plockton village, standing on a sheltered bay afloat with yachts and studded with tiny islands, is postcard-pretty; and the last stretch of line, along the coast from Duirinish to Erbusaig Bay and Kyle of Lochalsh, is perhaps the prettiest of all, with the small islands of Raasay, Scalpay, Longay and Pabay silhouetted on the western horizon. The Drambuie estate between Plockton and Duirinish lends its name to one of the world's favourite whisky-based liqueurs. Drambuie is said to be made from a secret recipe given to the local laird – a loyal Jacobite – before he fled to Skye after defeat at Culloden.

The line continues southwest, arriving after 15 minutes at Kyle of Lochalsh.

5 Kyle of Lochalsh

Kyle of Lochalsh is the end of the line in every sense of the word. This unassuming little village was, until the completion of the controversial road bridge to Skye in the 1990s, the mainland end of the main ferry crossing to Scotland's best-known island. The views from here across to Skye are spectacular and tempting, and most visitors prefer to travel on to Skye rather than to stay in Kyle of Lochalsh itself.

There are onward bus connections at Kyle for Skye (via road bridge) and ferries to the Western Isles. Buses also link Kyle of Lochalsh with Fort William and Inverness.

Tour: Inverness to Kyle of Lochalsh by train

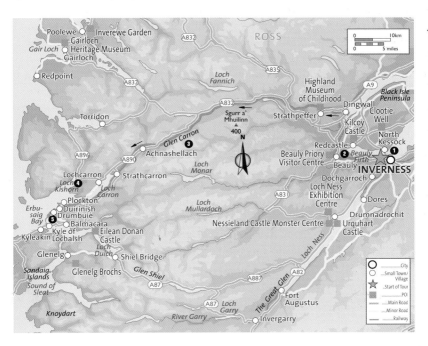

Loch Ness

The River Ness flows through Inverness from Loch Ness, which stretches some 36.4km (22²/₃ miles) southwest from Inverness through the Great Glen. At its deepest, the loch is 213m (700ft) in depth and it is the largest volume of fresh water in Britain. The Caledonian Canal links the loch with Loch Lochy and Loch Linnhe in Argyll, connecting the Moray Firth with the Atlantic. The small village of Drumnadrochit, on the north shore of Loch Ness, is the hub of a thriving tourism and souvenir industry inspired by the myth of the Loch Ness Monster, locally known as 'Nessie'. Several companies operate sightseeing cruises on the loch, and some have boats equipped with sonar to search for signs of the monster. Motor cruisers and canal cruisers can also be hired for trips on the loch and the Caledonian Canal.

Loch Ness Exhibition Centre

This award-winning, long-established visitor attraction opened more than 30 years ago and has grown into a high-

The ruins of Urquhart Castle

Visitors scour the lake for a glimpse of Nessie

tech, multimedia presentation which also includes as much about the history and natural environment of the region. *Drumnadrochit, 24km (15 miles) southwest of Inverness on the A82. Tel: (01456) 450 573. www.lochness.com. Open: Feb–May & Oct daily 9.30am–5pm; Jun & Sept daily 9am–6pm; Jul–Aug daily 9am–6.30pm; Nov–Jan daily 10am–3.30pm. Admission charge.*

Nessieland Castle Monster Centre

'We believe in the monster', proclaim the owners of this visitor attraction and adventure playground on the shores of the loch. The exhibition includes records of purported 'sightings' of 'Nessie', while the activity centre features winding woodland paths with climbing frames, slides and a basket swing. *Drumnadrochit, 24km (15 miles) southwest of Inverness on the A82.*

Tel: (01456) 450 342. www.loch-ness-monster-nessieland.com. Open: Jun–Aug daily 9am–10pm; Sept–Oct daily 9am–8pm; Nov–May daily 9am–5pm. Admission charge.

Urquhart Castle

Built more than five centuries ago, this is one of Scotland's largest and most picturesque historic strongholds, with a spectacular location beside Loch Ness. Its most dramatic feature is the five-storey Grant Tower, where its noble owners lived and entertained, and the kitchens, guardhouse and cellars can also be visited. *3km (2 miles) southwest of Drumnadrochit on the A82. Tel: (01456) 450 551. Open: Apr–Sept daily 9.30am–6pm; Oct daily 9.30am–5pm; Nov–Mar daily 9.30am–4.30pm. Last admission 45 mins before closing. Admission charge.*

Drive: The Great Glen

This 96km (60-mile) drive follows the Caledonian Canal through the spectacular landscapes of the Great Glen, with its chain of deep, narrow lochs between steep hillsides. This drive is best between June and September, but traffic can be heavy during the July and August peak tourism season.

Allow half a day.

Leave Inverness by the A82. The road runs roughly parallel to the Caledonian Canal before reaching Loch Ness.

1 The Caledonian Canal and Loch Ness

Designed by the great 19th-century engineer Thomas Telford, and completed in 1822, the Caledonian Canal links Inverness and Loch Ness with the other lochs of the Great Glen to cut between the east and west coasts.

Loch Ness is narrow, deep and dark and it is easy to believe that there might be something lurking in its waters.
Continue for just over 23km (14 miles) on the A82 to Drumnadrochit village.

2 Drumnadrochit

Drumnadrochit makes its living from the 'monster industry'. Cruises also depart from this lochside village.
Continue along the A82 and the north shore of the loch for a further 3km (2 miles) to Urquhart Castle.

3 Urquhart Castle

Built around 1500, Urquhart Castle is one of Scotland's most picturesque ruins (*see p97*).

After a further 31km (19 miles), the A82 reaches Fort Augustus.

4 Fort Augustus

Like Fort George, this was once a military garrison town. Its main attraction is the **Canal Heritage Visitor Centre**, which describes the building of the Caledonian Canal.
Ardchattan House, Canalside, Fort Augustus. Tel: (01320) 366 493. www.scottishcanals.co.uk. Open: Apr–Oct daily 9.30am–5.30pm. Closed: Nov–Mar. Just 8km (5 miles) after leaving Fort Augustus, the A82 reaches the northeast end of Loch Oich. Just after Invergarry, look out for signs pointing to the Well of Seven Heads.

5 Well of Seven Heads

This monument commemorates seven men, executed here in the 17th century for the murder of two sons of a local chieftain.
From the south end of Loch Oich it's about 1.6km (1 mile) to Loch Lochy.

Continue for about 14km (8¾ miles). At Invergloy, the A82 deviates inland. Follow it for 4.8km (3 miles) to just before Spean Bridge.

6 Commando Memorial

This is dedicated to Britain's special forces soldiers who trained around Fort William during World War II. The statue was sculpted in 1952 by Scott Sutherland.

Follow the A82 for a further 15.5km (9²/₃ miles).

7 Inverlochy Castle

This castle was built in the 13th century by the Comyn family.

Inverlochy Castle. Tel: (01667) 460 232. Open: times vary – call for information. Admission charge.

Turn right on the A830 to Banavie.

8 Neptune's Staircase

This series of eight locks raises the canal's level by a total of 19.5m (64ft).

Turn around and follow the A830 back to the A82, then turn right to Fort William.

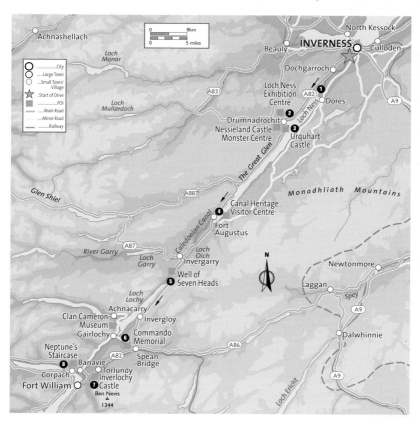

Something in the loch?

Scotland's largest and rarest animal is, of course, the legendary Loch Ness Monster. For some 75 years, since the first modern 'sighting' of the monster, Nessie has fascinated people worldwide, attracting thousands of visitors to the area in the hope of catching a glimpse of this elusive beast.

In and around Inverness, the myth of the Loch Ness Monster is big business. It generates hundreds of thousands of pounds a year from visitor centres, exhibitions, souvenirs, books and CDs, fluffy toys and postcards. So it's not surprising that most locals assert firmly that there is something huge and mysterious living in the loch, despite the notable lack of evidence for the claim.

Modern 'sightings' started in earnest in the 1930s, when a new road made the north shore of the loch accessible to more visitors, but the famous 'surgeon's photograph' of 1934, which seems to show a large creature with a humped back and long neck in the water, has been exposed as a hoax. Professional and amateur monster hunters have

Dusk across Loch Ness from the beach at Dores

A fibreglass model of Nessie at the visitor centre

deployed everything from echo-location equipment to remote-controlled, unmanned submersibles, but have so far failed to find so much as a blip, a bubble or the fleeting image of a fin.

But legends of a creature in Loch Ness go far back in time. Almost 1,500 years ago, St Columba, who brought Christianity to Scotland, was credited with saving the people round the loch from the depredations of a water monster, which he put to flight by the power of prayer and the Cross. This sounds very much like early Christian propaganda, but water monsters known as 'kelpies' or 'water

horses' appear in many Gaelic folk tales. And similar lake creatures have been reported from all over the world, from Loch Morar on the Scottish west coast to Scandinavia, Canada and Cameroon.

If Nessie is real, what might she be? Bernard Heuvelmans, the Belgian father of 'cryptozoology' (the study of unknown animals), speculated that Nessie could be anything from a giant otter, an ancient species of long-necked whale, some kind of large seal – or even a huge eel.

The image that has captured the popular imagination since the 'surgeon's photograph' was taken is of a last survival from the days of the dinosaurs. Sadly, this attractive explanation is also the least plausible. The last of the long-necked sea reptiles – known as plesiosaurs – died out hundreds of millions of years ago. It is deeply improbable that any could have lived on in these Highland waters.

But the search for Nessie goes on, and the money keeps rolling in. Loch Ness is dark, and has an average depth of 130m (427ft), and nothing will persuade true believers in monsters that it holds no secrets. After all, as they say, absence of evidence is not evidence of absence. Maybe, after all, the truth is still out there somewhere.

The Northwest Highlands

Northwest of the Great Glen lies a vast and thinly populated region of heather-covered moors, silver lochs and streams, isolated glens and steep hills that may be capped with snow even in early summer. To the west, the Atlantic coastline is fringed with deep sea lochs and sweeping white-sand bays, and throughout the region the castles – some in ruins, some still inhabited – of Highland chieftains recall the glory days of the clans.

Ardnamurchan

Between the Sound of Arisaig to the north and the mouth of Loch Sunart to the south, the Ardnamurchan Peninsula stretches westward to the most westerly point of mainland Britain. The single-lane B8007 road runs along the south coast of the peninsula, connecting its main village, Kilchoan, with Strontian at the head of Loch Sunart.
Kilchoan is 80km (50 miles) west of Fort William.

Ardnamurchan Point Visitor Centre

The 36m (117ft) stone lighthouse tower that dominates Ardnamurchan Point was built in 1849. It is still a working lighthouse, but is now fully automated. The visitor centre is housed in the former head keeper's house, and visitors can also see the old engine room and foghorn. The views from here of the Inner Hebrides and the Small Isles are amazing.
Ardnamurchan Point, 10km (6¼ miles) west of Kilchoan on the B8007.

Tel: (01972) 510 210.
www.ardnamurchanlighthouse.com.
Open: May–Oct daily 10am–5pm.
Guided tours hourly 11am–4.30pm.
Booking essential. Closed: Nov–Apr.
Admission charge.

Arisaig

The Arisaig region stretches from Glenfinnan and Loch Shiel to the Sound of Arisaig on the west coast. Arisaig village, on a shallow bay at the western tip of this peninsula, is the best base for exploring this part of the Highlands. A string of excellent white-sand beaches stretches for some 13km (8 miles) north of Arisaig to the tiny village of Morar, on the coast close to the west end of Loch Morar.
56km (35 miles) west of Fort William on the A830.

Arisaig Land, Sea and Islands Centre

This small but interesting exhibition highlights aspects of the area ranging from crofting, fishing, folklore and social history to the world of the Special Operations Executive agents who trained in Arisaig during World War II for secret missions.

Arisaig village centre. Tel: (07973) 252 923. www.arisaigcentre.co.uk. Open: Apr–Oct Mon–Fri 10am–4pm, Sun 1–4pm. Closed: Nov–Mar & Sat. Admission charge.

Assynt

The Assynt region, which extends approximately from Loch Broom northwards to Cape Wrath, is one of the most remote and beautiful places in Britain – an area of sandy bays dotted with tiny islands, steep peaks rising from heathery moors, and dozens of silvery tarns and lochans. At its heart lies Loch Assynt, overlooked by the summits of Quinag, Suilven and Ben More Assynt. The village of **Lochinver**, overlooking Enard Bay, is the tourism 'capital' of the region, with a handful of places to stay and eat and a visitor centre.

160km (100 miles) northwest of Inverness on the A837. Tourist Information Office: Kirk Lane, Lochinver. Tel: (0845) 22 55 121. www.visitscotland.com.
Assynt Visitor Centre: Main Street, Lochinver. Tel: (01571) 844 373. www.assynt.info. Open: Easter–May Mon–Sat 10am–5pm; Jun–Sept daily 10am–5pm. Closed: Oct–Easter. Free admission.

Achiltibuie Hydroponicum (Garden of the Future)

In the tiny village of Achiltibuie, on the south coast of the Coigach Peninsula and looking out towards the tiny Summer Isles and Gruinard Bay, this high-tech, organic indoor garden is a 21st-century creation where subtropical and temperate-zone trees, flowers, herbs and vegetables flourish in the unlikely surroundings of Scotland's far north.

Achiltibuie, 32km (20 miles) south of Lochinver. Tel: (01854) 622 202.

www.thehydroponicum.com.
Open: Easter–Sept daily 10am–6pm;
Oct Mon–Fri noon–2pm.
Closed: Nov–Easter. Admission charge.

Ardvreck Castle

Assynt is MacLeod territory, and this romantic 13th-century ruin beside Loch Assynt was one of their strongholds. The Royalist commander Montrose fled to Assynt after his defeat by Cromwell's Parliamentarians at Bonar Bridge in 1650, was captured, and then imprisoned here before being sent to Edinburgh, where they chopped off his head.
18km (11 miles) east of Lochinver on the A837. Open: daily, dawn until dusk. Free admission.

Handa Island

Shags, fulmars, guillemots and razorbills nest in their thousands on the 350m (1,150ft) cliffs and peat bogs of this tiny island, which is run as a seabird sanctuary by the Scottish Wildlife Trust. Seals also abound in the surrounding waters. Handa has been uninhabited since 1846, when most of the islanders emigrated to Canada to escape starvation during the potato famine that afflicted the Highlands at the time.
10km (6 miles) northwest of Scourie. Tel: (01463) 714 746. www.swt.org.uk. Open: Apr–Sept Mon–Sat. Shuttle passenger-only ferries (no cars) leave Tarbet Pier 6km (4 miles) north of Scourie from 9.30am to 2pm, last return journey 5pm, crossing time 30 mins. Closed: Oct–Mar. Admission charge.

Scourie

Scourie, on the north shore of the beautiful Edrachillis Bay, has no visitor attractions as such, but overlooks a fine, sandy beach. There are a few places to stay (including a camping and caravan site) and eat in, around the village, and ferries leave from the even tinier settlement of Tarbet, 6km (4 miles) north of Scourie, for the Handa Island bird sanctuary (*see above*).
72km (45 miles) north of Ullapool on the A894.

Suilven

At 731m (2,399ft), Suilven is not the highest summit in the Assynt area, but it is the most challenging and spectacular, and the view from the summit, looking north over Assynt and west towards the coast, is extraordinary.
16km (10 miles) southeast of Lochinver.

Cape Wrath

Cape Wrath, the northernmost point of the west coast, is wonderfully dramatic, with the Clo Mor cliffs (Britain's highest sea cliffs) plunging 280m (920ft) into the sea below.
20km (12 miles) northwest of Durness.

Durness

Durness, nestling above a sandy bay, is the most northwesterly village in mainland Britain. Its other claim to fame is that John Lennon holidayed here as a child. Just outside the village is the spectacular Smoo Cave (*see below*). *40km (25 miles) northeast of Scourie on the A838.*

Smoo Cave

Some 60m (200ft) long and 30m (100ft) wide at the entrance, this enormous sea cave is one of the largest caverns in Britain. A wooden walkway leads into the cave; archaeologists have found evidence that Stone Age people once lived here.
800m (½ mile) east of Durness, off the A838. No tel. Email: info@smoocave.org. www.smoocave.org. Open: Apr–May daily 11am–4pm; Jun–Sept daily 10am–5pm. Closed: Oct–Mar. Admission charge.

Eilean Donan Castle

Built in 1214, Eilean Donan is the archetypal Highland castle and has appeared in countless films, postcards, posters and advertising campaigns. Once the seat of the Mackenzie lairds of Kintail, it was shelled into rubble by the Royal Navy in the brief Jacobite rising of 1719, when a small garrison of Spanish troops was stranded here. It lay in ruins for almost two centuries until it was bought in 1911 by Colonel John MacRae-Gilstrap, who spent the next 20 years repairing it. It has been the home of his descendants ever since.
Loch Duich, 13km (8 miles) east of Kyle of Lochalsh on the A87. Tel: (01599) 555 202. www.eileandonancastle.com. Open: mid-Mar–Jun & Sept–mid-Nov daily

Eilean Donan Castle on the edge of Loch Duich

10am–6pm; Jul–Aug daily 9am–6pm.
Last admission 5pm. Closed: mid-
Nov–mid-Mar. Admission charge.

Gairloch

Gairloch village faces south across Gair Loch, a scenic west-facing bay, and stretches along a fine sandy shore for around 3km (2 miles). It is home to a couple of small visitor attractions and a reasonable choice of accommodation and places to eat. From its harbour, boats can be rented for sea-fishing trips, and other activities include seal- and dolphin-spotting cruises, walking and pony trekking.
113km (70 miles) northwest of Inverness on the A832.

Gairloch Heritage Museum

Old wooden fishing boats, a reconstruction of a crofter's home and the old village schoolroom, the old dairy and village shop are among the interesting exhibits here, which also include archaeological relics going all the way back to the Stone Age.
Achtercairn, Gairloch village centre. Tel: (01445) 712 287.
www.gairlochheritagemuseum.org.uk.
Open: Apr–Oct Mon–Sat 10am–5pm.
Open by arrangement Nov–Mar.
Admission charge.

Gairloch Marine Life Centre

This visitor centre has impressive displays and videos of whales, dolphins, porpoises and other local sea creatures, as well as footage of golden eagles, the recently reintroduced white-tailed sea eagle, and many other seabirds. In summer, there are also whale- and dolphin-spotting cruises escorted by local experts.
Gairloch Harbour, Pier Road, Gairloch. Tel: (01445) 712 636.

Exotic planting survives well at Inverewe Garden

www.porpoise-gairloch.co.uk.
Open: Mon–Fri 10am–3pm, Sat–Sun
11am–3pm. Admission charge.

Inverewe Garden
Victorian horticulturalist and landscape
architect Osgood Mackenzie created this
astonishing garden of exotic plants
beside Loch Ewe, importing subtropical
plants – including palm trees – that
flourish in this northern setting thanks
to a clement microclimate created by its
position on the edge of the Gulf Stream.
*Poolewe, 10km (6 miles) northeast of
Gairloch on the A832. Tel: (01445) 781
200. www.nts.org.uk. Open: Apr–May &
Sept daily 10am–5pm; Jun–Aug daily
10am–6pm; Oct daily 10am–4pm;
Nov–Mar daily 10am–3pm. Visitor
centre open: Easter–Sept daily
9.30am–5pm. Closed: Oct–Easter.
Admission charge.*

Glenelg Brochs
These two stone towers are among the
finest examples of Iron Age brochs
found on the Scottish mainland.
Unique to northwest Scotland, these
remarkable dry stone buildings are
attributed to the ancient Picts, but their
purpose remains a mystery.
*13km (8 miles) southeast of Kyle of
Lochalsh. Tel: (01667) 460 232.
www.historic-scotland.gov.uk.
Open: daily, dawn until dusk.*

Glenfinnan
Glenfinnan village sits midway between
Fort William and the west coast, at the

The Jacobite steam train crosses the Glenfinnan
Viaduct

northern end of long, narrow Loch
Shiel, and is best known for being
home to one of Britain's most
spectacular railway viaducts.

The 21 arches of the Glenfinnan
Viaduct, just north of Glenfinnan
village, will be immediately familiar
to anyone who has watched the *Harry
Potter* films, since the train that carries
the young wizard and his pals
to Hogwarts Academy steams across
this spectacular railway bridge on the
West Highland Line, built in 1901.
*On the A830, 30km (19 miles) west of
Fort William.*

Glenfinnan Monument
Alexander MacDonald of Glenaladale
had this monument to the losers of the
1745–6 Jacobite rising built in 1815, on
the spot where Charles Edward Stuart

raised his colours in August 1745. The visitor centre recounts the sorry tale of the events that followed, from the Jacobite invasion of England to the Battle of Culloden and Charles's ignominious flight through the Highlands and escape to France.
1.6km (1 mile) east of Glenfinnan village on the A830. Tel: (01397) 722 250. www.nts.org.uk. Open: daily. Visitor centre: Glenfinnan. Open: Apr–Jun & Sept–Oct daily 10am–5pm; Jul–Aug daily 9.30am–5.30pm. Closed: Nov–Mar. Admission charge.

Glenfinnan Station Museum

This small museum tells the story of the building of the West Highland Line, arguably the most spectacularly picturesque stretch of railway line in Britain.
Glenfinnan Station, Glenfinnan village centre. Tel: (01397) 722 295.

The port of Mallaig

www.glenfinnanstationmuseum.co.uk. Open: Jun–mid-Oct daily 9am–5pm. Closed: mid-Oct–May. Admission charge.

Mallaig

The small port of Mallaig sits on the west coast of Morar, and while Mallaig itself is less than lovely, it is a bustling gateway to the wild region that straddles landlocked Loch Morar and lies south of Loch Nevis. This deep, narrow and curving sea loch stretches inland for some 16km (10 miles) from the Sound of Sleat, which separates the Isle of Skye from the mainland. Like Loch Ness, Loch Morar is claimed to be home to a monster – nicknamed 'Morag' – but the evidence is equally slim. Mallaig is also the port for ferries shuttling across to Armadale on the Isle of Skye, and to its smaller neighbours, Rhum, Eigg and Muck (*see p120*).
72km (45 miles) northwest of Fort William on the A830.

Mallaig Heritage Centre

Displays outline the history of the northwest's fishing and crafting industries, the arrival of the railway that turned Mallaig into a busy transit point, and the social history of Morar and the neighbouring Knoydart region.
Station Road, Mallaig. Tel: (01687) 462 292. www.mallaigheritage.org.uk. Open: Apr–mid-Jul & Oct Mon–Sat 11am–4pm; mid-Jul–Sept Mon–Sat 9.30am–4.30pm, Sun 12.30–4.30pm. Closed: Nov–Mar. Admission charge.

Ullapool

The largest town in the northwest, Ullapool is also the newest – it was built from scratch in 1788 as a herring fishing port. It's the main port for ferries to Stornoway, on the Isle of Lewis in the Outer Hebrides, and is also a busy fishing harbour. On the north shore of Loch Broom, Ullapool is also the jumping-off point for cruises to the scenic Summer Isles, in Gruinard Bay.
98km (61 miles) northwest of Inverness on the A835.

Rhue Settlement

Circles of stones and low earth mounds mark the site of this prehistoric village of ancient 'round houses', which may be dated as early as 1500 BC, making it one of the oldest settlement sites in the Highland region.
Off the A835 (signposted), 4km (2½ miles) north of Ullapool. No tel. www.ullapool.co.uk. Open: all year daily 24 hours (unenclosed). Free admission.

Ullapool Museum and Visitor Centre

The museum focuses on the history of Ullapool and its fishing industry, as well as its role as an emigrant port from which thousands of Highlanders left Scotland during the Clearances.
*7–8 West Argyle Street, Ullapool.
Tel: (01854) 612 987.
www.ullapoolmuseum.co.uk.
Open: Apr–Oct Mon–Sat 10am–5pm.
Closed: Nov–Mar & Sun.
Admission charge.*

A ferry from Stornoway arrives in Ullapool

The Northeast Highlands

The Northeast Highlands, from the north shore of the Moray Firth to the northernmost point in mainland Britain, do not have the obvious appeal of the northwest. The North Sea coast can be bleak, and the region lacks the spectacular sea lochs, glens and mountains of the northwest. Nevertheless, the brooding moorlands of Caithness's Flow Country have a stark grandeur, and the region has a number of historic sights that are worth a visit.

The Black Isle

So called because its pine-wooded slopes make it appear dark when seen from Inverness, the Black Isle is not an island at all, but a peninsula, between the Moray Firth to the south and the Cromarty Firth in the north. The new Kessock suspension bridge across the narrows of the Moray Firth connects it with Inverness.

Cromarty, on the northern tip of the peninsula, is the Black Isle's main town. *North Kessock Tourist Information Centre: north side of Kessock Bridge, off the northbound carriageway of the A9, 5km (3 miles) north of Inverness. Tel: (0845) 22 55 121. Open: May–Jun Mon–Sat 10am–5pm, Sun noon–5pm; Jul–Aug Mon–Sat 10am–5.30pm, Sun 11am–5.30pm; Sept–Oct Mon–Sat 10am–4pm. Closed: Nov–Apr.*

Clootie Well

This wishing well is a weird survival of ancient Highland superstition. The trees around it are festooned with rags, and folklore claims that to have a wish granted you must spill three drops of water, tie a rag to a handy branch, cross yourself, then take a drink from the well. The well is said to be dedicated to St Boniface, but the ritual seems to be at least partly pre-Christian. *Munlochy, 8km (5 miles) north of Inverness.*

Cromarty Courthouse Museum

Built in 1773, the old courthouse is now a museum with tours of the cells, a re-enactment of an 18th-century trial, and displays of 18th- and 19th-century costume. *Church Street, Cromarty, 40km (25 miles) north of Inverness on the A832. Tel: (01381) 600 418. www.cromarty-courthouse.org.uk. Open: Apr–Oct daily 10am–5pm. Closed: Nov–Mar. Admission charge.*

Fortrose Cathedral

Fortrose's 13th-century cathedral is very ruined, but the surviving parts, including the vaulted undercroft of the chapter house and part of the 14th-century nave, show fine workmanship. *Fortrose village centre, 16km (10 miles) northeast of Inverness. Tel: (01667) 460 232. Open: daily, dawn until dusk.*

North Kessock Dolphin and Seal Centre

The red kite was reintroduced into Scotland in the 1990s and these beautiful raptors now breed successfully on the Black Isle. Closed-circuit TV cameras allow close-up views of nesting birds and their young without disturbing them, and the centre also offers seal- and dolphin-spotting cruises. *Tel: (01463) 731 866. www.wdcs.org. Open: Jun–Sept daily 9.30am–12.30pm & 1–4.30pm. Closed: Oct–May.*

Dornoch and the Dornoch Firth

The douce golfing town and summer resort of Dornoch looks south over the Dornoch Firth, a deep inlet of the North Sea, to the Whiteness Sands and

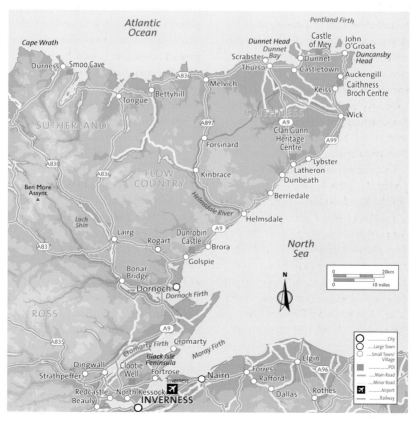

Tarbat Ness on the other side of the Firth. It claims to be one of Scotland's sunniest towns, and miles of sands attract hardy swimmers and windsurfers in summer. Dornoch's golf course is rated one of the world's best. Founded in the 12th century, the town centre is graced by a handful of medieval buildings, most of which have been extensively restored.
On the A9, 64km (40 miles) north of Inverness.

Dornoch Cathedral

Founded in 1224, the cathedral was almost completely destroyed by fire in 1570. In 1835, it was enthusiastically restored by the Countess of Sutherland; a second, more sensitive restoration, in 1924, returned it to a state closer to its medieval original. The stained-glass windows were a gift from the Scots-American millionaire philanthropist Andrew Carnegie.
The Square, Dornoch. Tel: (01862) 810 357. www.dornoch-cathedral.com. Open: daily 9am–dusk. Donations welcome.

Historylinks Museum

This excellent museum traces Dornoch's history from the era of the Picts and Vikings, through the clan feuds of the 15th and 16th centuries (when the Mackays burnt the cathedral and much of the town), to the 19th century, the coming of the railway and the development of the town into a magnet for golfers.
The Meadows, Dornoch. Tel: (01862) 811 275. www.historylinks.org.uk. Open: Easter week & Jun–Sept daily 10am–4pm; Apr–May & Oct Mon–Fri

The immaculately tended gardens of Dunrobin Castle

10am–4pm; Nov–Mar Wed–Thur
10am–4pm. Admission charge.

Witch's Stone

This stone commemorates the
execution by burning – in 1722 – of
Janet Horne, the last woman to be
convicted of witchcraft in Scotland.
Carnaig Street, The Square, Dornoch.

Helmsdale

The present-day fishing port of
Helmsdale was founded in the second
half of the 19th century as a new home
for crofters evicted from the nearby
glens during the notorious Highland
Clearances, and stands on the site of a
much older Viking settlement dating
back to around the 10th century AD.
Helmsdale is an attractive village of
neat grey-stone houses and cottages
around the harbour, and is well
supplied with places to eat and stay.
Inland, gold has been found – albeit in
tiny, uncommercial quantities – in the
River Helmsdale, which meets the sea
here and is popular with trout and
salmon fishermen.
*113km (70 miles) north of Inverness on
the A9 coast road.*

Dunrobin Castle

Dunrobin Castle has been the seat of
the earls and dukes of Sutherland since
1401, but the grandiose pile that now
stands here, amid splendid formal
gardens overlooking the North Sea,
dates from the mid-19th century,
when it was extensively rebuilt.

Dornoch Sands, on the north coast of Dornoch
Firth

Within is an opulent collection of
portraits, landscape paintings and
antique furniture, and a museum
dedicated to the history of the
Sutherland region and the ducal
family. There are falconry displays
featuring golden eagles and peregrine
falcons, and a shop and tearoom for
light meals and snacks.
*Off the A9, 1.6km (1 mile) north Golspie.
Tel: (01408) 633 177.
www.dunrobincastle.co.uk.
Open: Mar–May & Sept–Oct Mon–Sat
10.30am–4.30pm (falconry displays
11.30am & 2pm), Sun noon–4.30pm
(no falconry displays); Jun–Aug daily
10.30am–5.30pm (falconry displays
11.30am & 2pm). Closed: Nov–Feb.
Admission charge.*

Timespan Heritage Centre

The exhibition explores the history of the local crofting communities and the struggle for land rights and fair rents in the 'Crofters' War' and also has a storytelling centre and a pretty herb garden.

Dunrobin Street, Helmsdale. Tel: (01431) 821 327. www.timespan.org.uk. Open: Mon–Sat 10am–5pm, Sun noon–5pm. Admission charge (museum).

John O'Groats

A visit to John O'Groats is almost compulsory when in this part of Scotland, but the village itself is an anticlimax. It is named after a Dutch ferryman, Jan de Groot, who carried passengers between here and Orkney in the 15th century. Although the northernmost point of the longest line between two spots of the mainland (the other being Land's End in Cornwall), the village is not in fact mainland Britain's northernmost point. That honour goes to Dunnet Head, 13km (8 miles) west of here.

A836, 32km (20 miles) east of Thurso. www.visitjohnogroats.com

Strathpeffer

Strathpeffer seems an unlikely location for a Victorian spa town, but during the 19th century its sulphur-laden springs with their supposedly therapeutic properties attracted large numbers of visitors. Relics of that era include a **Spa Pavilion** – restored to its former glory – and the Pump Room, where visitors

can sniff and sip at the foul-tasting medicinal waters.

24km (15 miles) northwest of Inverness on the A834.
Spa Pavilion: The Square. Tel: (01997) 420 124. www.strathpefferpavilion.org

Highland Museum of Childhood

Housed in the town's restored Victorian railway station, the museum focuses on childhood in the Highlands in bygone times, with collections of toys, dolls and games.

The Old Station, Strathpeffer. Tel: (01997) 421 031. www.highlandmuseumofchildhood.org. uk. Open: Apr–Jun & Sept–Oct Mon–Sat 10am–5pm, Sun 2–5pm; Jul–Aug Mon–Fri 10am–7pm, Sat 10am–5pm, Sun 2–5pm. Closed: Nov–Mar. Admission charge.

Thurso

Thurso dates from Viking times and had Scandinavian connections in medieval times, too, exporting oatmeal, fish and beef. Its main importance today is as a commercial town and a gateway to the Orkney Islands, with ferries sailing from its port of Scrabster, a mile northwest of the town centre.

Castle of Mey

Built in the late 16th century by George Sinclair, the fourth Earl of Caithness, the castle was occupied by his descendants for three centuries. After the death of the 15th earl in 1889, it lay derelict until it was acquired by the

Queen Mother in 1952. In 1996, she transferred ownership to the Castle of Mey Trust. It has a traditional walled garden and an animal centre with rare breeds of pig, poultry and sheep.
On the A836, 23km (14 miles) east of Thurso. Tel: (01847) 851 473. www.castleofmey.org.uk. Open: 1 May– 30 Jul & 13 Aug–30 Sept daily 10.30am–5pm. Last admission 4pm. Closed: 31 Jul–12 Aug & Oct–Apr. Admission charge.

Dunnet Head
This 127m (417ft) sandstone headland is the true northernmost point of mainland Britain and is much more impressive than John O'Groats, with breathtaking views across the Pentland Firth to Orkney.
19km (12 miles) northeast of Thurso on the B855.

Thurso Heritage Museum
The most interesting elements of this museum's collection are the Pictish symbol-stones, with their carvings of legendary beasts, birds and fish.
Town Hall, High Street. Tel: (01847) 892 692. Open: Mon–Sat 11am–8pm, Sun 11am–4pm. Free admission.

The Northeast Highlands

The walled garden of the Castle of Mey, former home of the Queen Mother

Walk: Castle of Mey to Castletown

This fairly easy 16km (10-mile) coastal walk over level roads and trails takes in a range of sights – from the impressive Castle of Mey via the stark promontory of Dunnet Head, with its spectacular views over the Pentland Firth, to the old flagstone quarry in Castletown. Buses link the start and end points of the walk to Thurso.

Allow around 4–5 hours.

Start this walk at Mey village, on the A836, 23km (14 miles) east of Thurso (there are regular buses from Thurso). From the bus stop at Mey village, walk 800m (½ mile) north to the gateway to Castle of Mey.

1 Castle of Mey

With its towers and corbelled turrets, the castle is immediately impressive. Built between 1566 and 1572, it was purchased by the Queen Mother in 1952 and gifted by her to the Castle of Mey Trust in 1996. Take time to visit the garden, protected from the North Sea gales by the Great Wall of Mey. *Leave the castle grounds, turn right, and follow the road for 800m (½ mile) as it curves northwest towards the coast, crossing a small stream, the Mey Burn, just before the village of Scarfskerry, overlooking the Pentland Firth.*

2 Scarfskerry

Scarfskerry is little more than a string of white-painted stone houses along a rocky shore, but it does claim the northernmost church on the British mainland. The village's name means 'shag rock' and derives from the *skerry* (rocky islet) just offshore on which these seabirds – called *scarfs* in old Caithness dialect – still roost.
Follow the country road southwest for about 2km (1¼ miles) to a T-junction and turn right. Follow the road towards the coast for 1km (²/3 mile), then continue for a further 1km (²/3 mile) through the hamlet of Brough before turning right on a slightly larger country road, the B855. Follow this for 3km (2 miles) to Dunnet Head.

3 Dunnet Head

Dunnet Head is not only further north than John O'Groats, but also further north than Moscow. From this craggy promontory you can see clear across the Pentland Firth to the islands of Orkney, Stroma and South Ronaldsay; its sea-sculpted sandstone cliffs are home to huge numbers of seabirds.

Retrace your steps towards Brough, forking right for Dunnet, and 2km (1¼ miles) before you reach the village, turn right for 1.6km (1 mile).

4 Mary-Ann's Cottage

Mary-Ann Calder's father built this crofter's cottage more than 150 years ago, and it has been maintained exactly as it was when she vacated it at the age of 93, in 1990.
Walk 180m (200 yards) south, to the north end of Dunnet Bay.

5 Dunnet Bay

This huge, windswept sandy beach is backed by massive sand dunes, and its breakers attract Britain's hardiest

surfers. Without a wetsuit, its waters are too chilly for comfort, but it's a marvellous place for beachcombing.
Follow the sands south for 2.8km (1¾ miles).

6 Castlehill Quarry and Flagstone Trail

The workings, harbour and buildings of a vast abandoned stone quarry lie at the south end of the bay. Caithness stone was a valued building material, and the Castlehill Flagstone Trail tells visitors about the industry that once supplied flagstones to cities all over the world.
Follow the waymarked Flagstone Trail for 180m (200 yards) south to Castletown village and the end of this walk.

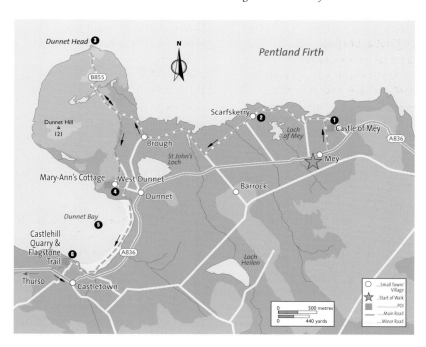

Wick

During the 19th century, Wick, situated on an east-facing bay close to the northernmost part of Scotland, flourished as the biggest herring-fishing port in the world and its catch was exported as far away as Russia and the Caribbean. Today, its fleet is much diminished, with only a handful of vessels compared with the 1,100 it once owned and its harbour is surrounded by the disused warehouses and barrel-making sheds that once supplied the fishing industry.

Caithness Broch Centre

This entertaining and educational new museum looks at the ancient and enigmatic stone towers known as brochs which are dotted around the Caithness landscape, as well as the

WHALES AND DOLPHINS

The Moray Firth, between the Black Isle and Inverness, has what is believed to be one of the largest populations of bottlenose dolphins in British waters, and is one of the best places in Scotland to spot a number of marine mammals. The dolphins are often seen close inshore at North Kessock, and they also range from the Firth up the North Sea coast. Harbour porpoises, the smallest of Britain's cetaceans, are also often spotted in the Moray Firth. Larger, more spectacular but less common are minke whales, which are sometimes seen in the Firth, and killer whales, also called orcas, which can be seen on the east and west coasts of the Scottish Highlands, and which gave their name to the Orkney Islands, just across the Pentland Firth from Caithness.

19th- and 20th-century scholars and amateur archaeologists who helped to uncover their secrets, and the lifestyle of the people who built them.

The lifeboat station at Wick

The Clan Gunn Heritage Centre at the parish church, Latheron

The Old School House, Auckengill, 16km (10 miles) north of Wick on the A99. Tel: (01955) 607 771. Open: Apr–Sept Mon–Fri 10.30am–4pm; Sat (Jul–Aug) 10.30am–4pm. Closed: Oct–Mar. Free admission.

Clan Gunn Heritage Centre

The centre tells the fascinating story of one of Scotland's oldest clans, with an ancient descent that fuses Norse and Celtic ancestry from the 9th century down to the present day.

Latheron, 26km (16 miles) southwest of Wick on the A9/A99. Tel: (01593) 741 700. Open: Jun–Sept Mon–Sat 11am–1pm & 2–4pm, (Aug) Sun 2–4pm. Closed: Oct–May. Admission charge.

Wick Heritage Centre

This award-winning museum contains a fascinating archive of photographs, films, documents and accessories from the heyday of Wick's fishing industry, including the lights, lenses and clockwork machinery from the former Noss Head lighthouse, which stood north of Wick. The museum's collection also includes the *Isabella Fortuna*, a lovingly restored sailing fishing vessel built in 1890, which is normally moored in Wick Harbour.

18–27 Bank Row, Pultneytown, Wick. Tel: (01955) 605 393. www.wickheritage.org. Open: Easter–Oct Mon–Sat 10am–3.45pm. Closed: Nov–Easter & Sun. Admission charge.

Getting away from it all

The islands of the Inner Hebrides – some large, some tiny – lie tantalisingly close to the mainland and are easy to get to by ferry, either for a day trip or for a longer stay. Empty Atlantic beaches haunted by gulls and kittiwakes, stupendous sunsets, and bays and sea lochs where seals, dolphins and whales can often be seen, are all aspects of their unique appeal. The Northern Isles offer a completely different landscape and are equally well worth a visit.

The Inner Hebrides

Separated from it by a series of narrow channels or sounds, the islands of the Inner Hebrides lie within sight of the mainland, and **Skye**, the largest and best known of the Hebridean islands, is now connected to the mainland by a new road bridge between Kyle of Lochalsh and Kyleakin. Skye's high-profile attraction is **Dunvegan Castle**, the ancient seat of the chiefs of the MacLeod clan for more than 800 years, while the steep peaks of the Cuillins, on the island's south coast, offer some of the most challenging hillwalking in Britain.

Further south, **Mull** is separated from the mainland by the Sound of Mull and the Firth of Lorn, with ferries from Oban to postcard-pretty **Tobermory**, where stone houses painted in pastel colours surround the harbour. Mull is reckoned to be one of the best places in Scotland for wildlife, with the chance of seeing red deer, golden eagles and the reintroduced white-tailed sea eagle, while in the waters around the island it is possible to spot minke whales, killer whales, porpoises, three species of dolphin (Risso's, common and bottlenose), grey and common seals and basking sharks. Mull also has two very different castles – medieval **Duart Castle**, seat of Clan MacLean, on its crag overlooking the Sound of Mull, and the 19th-century baronial pile of **Torosay**, set amid immaculately laid-out gardens. Off Mull's western tip, the tiny, tranquil island of **Iona** is a spiritual retreat, originally established by St Columba, who founded Scotland's first Christian mission here in the 7th century AD. Between Mull and Skye, an archipelago of smaller, remoter isles – **Eigg**, **Muck**, **Rhum**, **Coll** and **Tiree** – offer even greater tranquillity, with wild and windswept beaches and rocky shorelines where puffins, kittiwakes, fulmars, guillemots and razorbills roost.

South of Mull, the islands of **Islay** and **Jura** – separated by the narrow

Sound of Islay – are famous for their distilleries. For lovers of great malt whisky, labels such as Lagavulin, Laphroaig and Bruichladdich are names to conjure with, and no visit to either island would be complete without visiting at least one of these historic makers of malt whisky for a distillery tour and a sampling session. But Islay is also a fantastic island for wildlife watching, with the possibility of seeing red deer stags locking antlers as they compete for mating territory, huge flocks of white-fronted geese on their annual transatlantic migratory flights, and many more rare bird species.

The Northern Isles

The islands of the Orkney archipelago, across the Pentland Firth from mainland Scotland's most northerly point, have a very different heritage from the isles of the Hebrides. Settled by Norsemen as early as the 9th century AD, their history was for centuries more closely linked with the Scandinavian

The small isles of Rhum, Eigg and Muck, seen from Ardnamurchan

Whale and dolphin cruises
Sea Life Surveys
Ledaig
Tobermory
Isle of Mull PA75 6NR
Tel: (01688) 302 916. www.sealifesurveys.com

Islay birding and wildlife tours
Islay Birding
The Old Byre
Main Street
Port Charlotte
Islay PA48 7TX
Tel: (01496) 850 010. www.islaybirding.co.uk

Day trips to Orkney
John O'Groats Ferries
John O'Groats
Caithness KW1 4YR
Tel: (01955) 611 353. www.jogferry.co.uk

Ferries to the Inner Hebrides
Caledonian MacBrayne
Ferry Terminal
Gourock PA19 1QP
Tel: 0800 066 5000. www.calmac.co.uk

from the wind and furnished with stone bed platforms, seats, tables and fireplaces, some of them even had running water. The grass-covered mound of Maes Howe concealed the largest chambered tomb in Britain. Built around 2000 BC, it seems to have remained untouched until it was looted by Orkney Vikings in the 12th century AD. The Norse looters left a remarkable collection of runic graffiti carved into the chamber walls.

Though mostly treeless, low-lying Mainland is remarkably neat and fertile compared with the more rugged landscapes of the Hebrides. Inland, the island is a patchwork of fields and sheep pastures, but its coastlines are often spectacular, and its windswept

Kirkwall, the capital of the Orkney Islands

world than with the rest of Scotland – indeed, they did not formally become part of Scotland until the 15th century. But long before the Vikings came, these islands were settled by Stone Age people who left an array of burial sites and ancient settlements such as **Skara Brae** and **Maes Howe**, both on **Mainland**, the largest of the Orkney islands. Reckoned to be some 5,000 years old, Skara Brae is the oldest known settlement in Europe; it lay hidden beneath sand dunes for some 4,500 years, until it was uncovered by a mighty gale in 1850. Its circular stone houses are far from primitive: sheltered

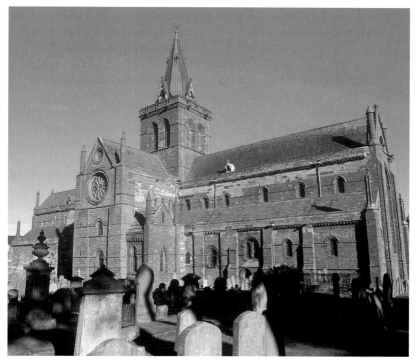

St Magnus Cathedral in Kirkwall, Mainland Orkney

cliffs support a unique variety of hardy plant life and thousands of seabirds. Birsay, in the northwest corner of Mainland, is home to the dramatic ruin of the **Earl's Palace**, built in the 16th century, while **St Magnus Cathedral**, in the centre of Kirkwall, the islands' capital, is one of the most impressive medieval buildings in Scotland.

South of Mainland, the island of **Hoy** is the second largest in the Orkney archipelago. Much of the island is covered by the North Hoy Reserve, run by the Royal Society for the Protection of Birds and providing a haven for skuas, snipe, peregrine falcons and mountain hares. Hoy's most striking natural feature is the famed **Old Man of Hoy**, a towering 'stack' or sandstone pinnacle that soars some 137m (450ft) from the sea. **Scapa Flow**, between Hoy and Mainland, is a superb natural anchorage that was the base of Britain's Grand Fleet during World War I and World War II. Beneath its waters lie the wrecks of 51 warships of the German Imperial Navy, scuttled in 1919 on the orders of their commanding officer to prevent them falling into the hands of the British.

When to go

Highland Scotland is a destination for all seasons, but it is at its best in early and late summer, at its least appealing from December to March, and at its most crowded in July and August. At any time of year, the visitor needs to be prepared for rain, wind and rapidly changing weather – a summer's day can begin with warm sun and cloudless skies and end with low cloud and driving rain.

The climate of the Scottish Highlands is significantly cooler and wetter than that of southern England. The temperature can drop below freezing at any time from October until April, and summer temperatures rarely rise much higher than 22°C (72°F). On high ground, winter temperatures can sometimes fall as low as −10°C (14°F); snow lies on higher peaks as late as June. Skiing is usually possible on the slopes of the Cairngorms and Glenshee from January until March or April and sometimes (as in 2010) until June. On high ground, weather is extremely changeable, and hillwalkers need to be prepared for heavy rain and low visibility even for a short walk in high summer, and to be aware of the risk of blizzards and gales in spring, autumn and winter.

However, the Highlands also have a very wide variety of microclimates. The Atlantic Current (the very tail end of the Gulf Stream) mellows the climate of the west coast, making it possible for subtropical plants and trees to flourish in parks and gardens as far north as Ullapool, but also makes for much heavier rainfall in western regions. The northeast coast, on the other hand, is drier but can be chillier than the west, with bitingly cold winds coming off the North Sea in winter and even in spring and early summer.

The weather can be glorious, but changeable

Northern Scotland in summer enjoys considerably longer hours of daylight than southern Britain; in the extreme north there is no complete darkness at midsummer. On the other hand, the Highlands have much shorter days in winter, with sunrise as late as 9.30am in midwinter, and darkness falling as early as 4pm.

The Highlands can be bleakly beautiful in midwinter, but the region is above all a destination for lovers of the outdoors, and harsh weather and the short hours of daylight are enough to discourage many visitors from December until Easter. In addition, many visitor attractions, guesthouses, hotels and activity operators are closed during the winter months. On balance, arguably the best times to visit are in early summer (late May and June) and late summer to early autumn (late August to early October). May is also one of the best times to see seabirds such as puffins, gannets and guillemots, which nest in large numbers on sea cliffs and offshore islands. Peak tourism season is from July to mid-August, when roads and attractions are crowded with visitors not only from abroad but from within Scotland, and accommodation is at a premium.

Scotland's northwest and north coasts have some of Europe's most beautiful beaches. Unlike those of the Mediterranean, they remain mostly pristine and undeveloped – and are likely to continue to be so, thanks to a climate that does not lend itself to

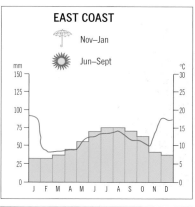

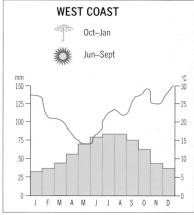

WEATHER CONVERSION CHART

25.4mm = 1 inch
°F = 1.8 × °C + 32

basking in the sun. That said, the waters of the west coast can be surprisingly clement in summer and watersports such as scuba diving, surfing and windsurfing are popular – keen surfers take to the breakers of beaches around Thurso even in winter.

Getting around

Getting around the Highlands without your own transport takes time and meticulous planning. Public transport is thin on the ground, especially in remoter areas of the northwest and Argyll.

Exploring the region by car is certainly the easy option, but it is possible to get almost everywhere using a combination of bus and train services if you are prepared to spend a little longer doing so.

Public transport information is easy to find on several websites and from a nationwide telephone and online information service, Traveline Scotland. Trains and buses are usually wheelchair accessible. Wheelchair-accessible taxis are also available at most railway and bus stations and airports, and on request when calling for a taxi. Other forms of public transport also cater well to those travellers who have disabilities.
Traveline Scotland. *Tel: (08712) 002 233. www.travelinescotland.com*

Buses

Long-distance buses connect the main towns and cities of the Highlands with Scotland's major cities. Mile for mile, bus travel is usually considerably cheaper than travelling by train, and local buses reach parts of the Highlands that are not served by trains. Bus services become further apart and fewer in remoter areas, and most smaller settlements have just two services a day, providing transport mainly for local schoolchildren.

Some small villages are served only by local postbuses that deliver the mail and carry up to ten fare-paying passengers. These make frequent stops, so they are a slow way to travel, but in parts of the Highlands the postbus is the only public transport option.

Driving

Bringing your own car to the Highlands is no problem. The M1/A1 east coast motorway connects London and southeast England with Edinburgh, from where the M90 motorway takes you to Perth in less than an hour's driving. From Perth, the A9 highway leads north through Pitlochry and Aviemore to Inverness, then onwards all the way up the northeast coast to Thurso.

The M6/A74/M74 route connects southern England with Glasgow, Scotland's largest city, from where the A82 leads north via Loch Lomond to

Fort William, then northeast through the Great Glen to Inverness. Off these major highways, roads can be steep and winding, and in remoter parts of Argyll and the northwest roads may be single-lane, with regular lay-bys or 'passing places' to allow vehicles coming in opposite directions to pass each other. Snow, ice and poor visibility are potential hazards from November to May. As in the rest of the UK, traffic drives on the left. Speed limits are 112km/h (70mph) on motorways, 96km/h (60mph) or 80km/h (50mph) on other highways and generally 48km/h (30mph), unless otherwise indicated, in built-up areas.

If travelling in winter, plan your journey to reach your destination before dark (which can be as early as 4pm), as driving and finding your way in darkness in winter conditions in the Highlands is no fun at all. The main providers of emergency breakdown services are the Automobile Association (AA) and Royal Automobile Club (RAC). Breakdown cover is normally included in the price of car rental.

Major car-hire companies have offices in Perth and Inverness. If you plan to fly to Scotland, then drive to the Highlands, you will find desks operated by all the main car-hire operators at Glasgow and Edinburgh airports. The minimum insurance required in the UK, whether with your own car or with a rented vehicle, is third-party liability coverage. In practice, when renting a

Be extra careful on single-track roads, especially in winter

car, the price will normally include this plus 'collision damage waiver' (CDW) insurance. However, this will also include an 'excess' provision, which may make you liable for a set amount if your rented vehicle is scratched, dented or stolen while in your charge. Read the small print on your contract carefully.

Taxis

Licensed taxis are readily available in most main towns in the Highlands, including Perth, Inverness, Fort William, Oban, Ullapool, Wick and Thurso, with taxi ranks at railway and bus stations and at Inverness Airport. Fares are metered and strictly controlled.

Ferries

As the old – and slightly resentful – west coast saying goes: 'God made the heavens and the Earth, and all that it contains; except the Highlands and the Isles, for they are all MacBrayne's.' And it is true that Caledonian MacBrayne has enjoyed a virtual monopoly of ferry services between the mainland and the islands of the Inner and Outer Hebrides ever since the 19th century. The company continues to be the main maritime transport provider between the Highlands and the Western Isles. The main ferry ports on the west coast are Oban, for services to Mull, Iona, Islay, Jura, Coll and Tiree; and Mallaig, for sailings to Skye, Rhum, Eigg and Muck.

A small vehicle ferry crosses the Narrows on Loch Linnhe

The ferryman helps cyclists board the ferry to the island of Lismore in Argyll

Three ferry companies provide services across the Pentland Firth from Caithness to Orkney. The shortest crossing is with the John O'Groats Ferry (40 mins) from John O'Groats but more convenient and frequent ferry services, connecting with trains and buses, are offered from Scrabster (the port of Thurso) by NorthLink Ferries and Pentland Ferries.

Caledonian MacBrayne
Ferry Terminal
Gourock PA19 1QP
Tel: 0800 066 5000. www.calmac.co.uk

John O'Groats Ferry
John O'Groats
Caithness KW1 4YR
Tel: (01955) 611 353. www.jogferry.co.uk

NorthLink Ferries
Kiln Corner, Ayre Road
Kirkwall KW15 1QX
Tel: 0845 6000 449.
www.northlinkferries.co.uk

Pentland Ferries
Pier Road, St Margaret's Hope
South Ronaldsay KW17 2SW
Tel: (01856) 831 226.
www.pentlandferries.co.uk

Trains
For those who are not in a hurry, travelling by train can be one of the most satisfying ways of exploring the Highlands. Trains become more infrequent as you head into remoter regions, but the view from your window is almost always spectacular, with some railway lines – such as the line across Rannoch Moor – traversing countryside that cannot be reached by road.

One main railway line snakes its way through northern Scotland from Perth through Pitlochry and Aviemore to Inverness, then up the northeast coast to Wick and Thurso. From Inverness and Perth there are also connections to London and all major UK cities.

On the west coast, trains run from Glasgow to Oban and Fort William. All local trains within the region are operated by **First ScotRail** and a range of flexible travel passes is available. *Tel: 0845 7484 950.*
www.scotrail.co.uk. Disabled assistance tel: 0800 912 2901.

Accommodation

The Scottish Highlands have an extremely wide range of accommodation, from camping and caravan sites to bijou guesthouses and ultra-luxurious hotels housed in historic buildings. The standard of accommodation has improved very considerably in recent years, and the Highlands now have a portfolio of places to stay that are as good as any in the world.

Prices, however, remain quite high in comparison with many other European destinations, mainly due to high operating costs and a relatively short summer holiday season. **VisitScotland** (*see page 133*) operates the Scottish Tourist Board grading scheme, which awards one to five stars to all types of accommodation. In one-star accommodation, you can expect a clean, tidy but basic room; two-star accommodation will be of a good all-round standard; three-star will show very good standards and attention to detail; and four- and five-star will be excellent to exceptional. VisitScotland also provides information on access for visitors with disabilities.

Camping, caravans and bothies

There are dozens of official camping and caravan sites in the Highlands, and the level of facilities varies widely. Most are open from April to October, but only the hardiest visitor will wish to sleep under canvas outside the summer months. Permanently parked caravans on serviced sites offer a higher level of comfort than camping and can be very affordable. Free camping in open country is permitted under Scotland's liberal public access laws. In practice, this means camping well away from private homes, livestock and cultivated farmland. Bothies are very basic shelters which can be found strategically located on a number of hillwalking routes. These are usually free but offer nothing more than a fireplace, four walls and a roof over your head, as they are really only intended as emergency shelter for walkers caught in bad weather. If you intend to use this kind of spartan accommodation, you will need to bring your own sleeping bag and foam mattress.

Guesthouses, B&Bs and inns

In much of the Highlands, the most common form of accommodation is in bed-and-breakfast ('B&B') rooms in private family homes, with accommodation for no more than half a dozen guests. In most B&Bs guests share bathrooms and WC, though a few may have en-suite facilities. Staying in this type of accommodation is generally cheaper than staying in a hotel. Guesthouses might be slightly more luxurious than B&B accommodation, offering en-suite rooms and a wider range of services, such as evening meals and afternoon tea in addition to breakfast.

Inns and restaurants with rooms can be found in many villages and rural locations. The standard of food and accommodation varies widely,

as do prices, and some of the more highly regarded establishments can be expensive.

Hostels and budget hotels

The Scottish Youth Hostel Association (SYHA) has a network of more than 60 hostels all over Scotland, including many in some of the most beautiful and remote spots in the Highlands as well as in towns and cities. Hostels may be small country cottages, historic mansions (including one huge, rambling Victorian castle) or modern, purpose-designed buildings. Many hostels offer private rooms with bunks, twin beds or double

Not a bad view – Invercoe Caravan Park in Glencoe

beds as well as standard bunks in shared dormitories.

At the more affordable end of the hotel range are small, owner-operated hotels which offer a basic range of services such as bar and restaurant, reception desk, porter and off-street car parking, with in-room facilities including TV and direct-dial telephone. There is also a growing number of no-frills, purpose-built budget hotels operated by large hotel chains and offering modern facilities at strategic locations such as major motorway junctions, airports and town centres. These do not usually have their own bar or restaurant, but are located close to such facilities. Staying at these, payment by credit card is usually required on arrival. These hotels make up for their lack of character in terms of convenience (especially if arriving somewhere late at night) and value for money.

Self-catering

For those planning to stay for a week or more in one spot, self-catering cottages can be excellent value for money, especially for families with children. Most cottages are available for a minimum rental of one week, and prices vary widely depending on location, level of facilities and the season. There are also a number of purpose-built holiday resorts offering accommodation in the countryside in modern wooden chalets that sleep up to six adults in comfort, with full

Self-catering accommodation beside Loch Melfort near Oban

The Kenmore Hotel, reputedly the oldest inn in Scotland

self-catering facilities. These complexes usually also have an on-site restaurant and bar and offer a range of open-air activities such as fishing, kayaking and cycling.

Town-house, luxury and specialist hotels

Town-house hotels – generally meriting a three- or four-star rating – are usually somewhat larger, with a high staff-to-guest ratio and professional management. Not all of them have a full-service bar and restaurant but most are located close to places to eat and drink.

At the higher end of the accommodation scale are some really luxurious hotels, many of which are housed in restored historic castles or 19th-century country mansions. These can be extremely expensive and exclusive, with a clientele that includes the rich and famous, world-class food, immaculate service, and frills such as state-of-the-art spas, private yachts and helicopter landing pads. In areas such as Tayside, Speyside and the northwest Highlands, there are also a number of

characterful anglers' hotels, dating from the 19th century. The best of these have their own trout and salmon fishing on lochs and rivers, and despite high prices there is often a waiting list for rooms in fishing season. Other specialist hotels include a number of golfing resort properties located on or near some of the best golf courses in the world.

VisitScotland also operates a nationwide accommodation booking and information service and publishes a range of brochures that list accommodation in all the regions of the Scottish Highlands. Be aware that many smaller establishments close between October and Easter, and that finding accommodation at short notice during the peak months of July and August can be tricky, so booking well in advance is strongly advisable. If you do arrive at your destination without having booked a place to stay, local tourist offices can usually help you to find a room.

VisitScotland booking and information service. *Tel: (0845) 22 55 121. www.visitscotland.com*

Food and drink

Since the 1990s, Scottish cooking has experienced a revolution, with Scottish chefs embracing new ways of preparing food while making the most of outstanding local produce. World-class restaurants can now be found in the most out-of-the-way places, and some are so highly regarded that visitors have to reserve a table months in advance. The list of acclaimed restaurants, bistros and gastro pubs grows longer year by year, ranging from gourmet establishments to simple pub-restaurants.

Until not so long ago, Scotland was seen as a bit of a culinary backwater, with an old-fashioned approach to dining. However, that began to change in the early 1990s, when a new generation of Scottish chefs took note of the country's superb larder of natural products.

Local produce

Despite the overfishing that has all but destroyed many fisheries, the west coast is still rich in seafood, and oysters, scallops, mussels, prawns, crab, lobster and salmon appear on many menus. There are concerns that some

operations, such as salmon farming, have an adverse effect on the marine environment, and there is increasing pressure on supermarkets and restaurants to use only seafoods that have been farmed sustainably or organically.

On land, Scotland also offers quality produce, including some of the world's best beef and lamb, and the number of farms producing organically raised meat is on the increase. Game shooting is still a popular (and expensive) pastime and – leaving aside the debate over the ethics of hunting and shooting – ensures that there is a plentiful supply of game meats such as grouse, pheasant and venison during the shooting season. Deer are also raised commercially, and organically farmed venison is available all year.

Changing attitudes to food

The eating habits that have changed the face of the smarter establishments of Scotland haven't yet generally

TIPPING

Tipping is not usual in self-service establishments such as pubs, bars and takeaway restaurants. A tip of around 10 per cent is appreciated by serving staff in more formal restaurants, hotel restaurants and bistro-bars, but even in these is not essential and should be used to reward exemplary service.

percolated down to street level. A remote Highland village may boast a Michelin-rated restaurant, but the local village shop is likely to stock only the usual processed, tinned and unperishable food items. Fish and chip shops, or 'chippers', are the culinary cornerstone of most village high streets, serving up the traditional takeaway items of battered fish, pies and pizzas.

Until the 19th century, the traditional diet of the Scottish Highlands was outstandingly healthy, rich in complex vegetable proteins from pulses, oats and

Fishing boats bring in the day's catch on the west coast at Kyleakin

A selection of Scottish seafood at Crannog at the Waterfront in Fort William

barley, high in oily fats and red meat – and almost entirely free of sugar.

By the 1840s, however, many Highland and Island communities had become overdependent on the potato (introduced to Scotland from the New World from around the 18th century), and failure of the potato crop in the mid-1840s caused hunger and even famine in remoter places. An even bigger change came with the Industrial Revolution, the Clearances, and the massive shift in population to the cities, where the children of crofters who had been turfed off their farmland grew up as factory workers, addicted to the novelties of sugar, tea, white bread and ready-made foods.

But Highlanders have become more adventurous in their eating habits. A generation ago, no one would have eaten squid – if caught they were either sold to make fertiliser or cat food, or simply dumped. Today, fried calamari is on most bar-bistro menus, along with an array of other dishes for which Scots have acquired a taste during their holidays in the sun. And on the high street of any sizeable town, there will be at least one Indian, Chinese or Thai restaurant competing with the indigenous chip shop.

Strict vegetarians are by and large not well catered for. More expensive eating places and sophisticated hotel restaurants generally offer a reasonable range of meat- and fish-free options. Smaller eating places may simply offer

SMOKING

Smoking was banned in all restaurants, bars, pubs and other indoor public spaces in Scotland in March 2006. As a result, hardened smokers can be seen huddled in pub and restaurant doorways while getting their nicotine fix, and many establishments offer a tiny outdoor space warmed by patio heaters so that smokers can sit outside.

omelettes, salads, vegetable soups and sandwiches.

Drink

The range of drinks available in Highland pubs varies widely – small village pubs will offer a choice of spirits and mixers and a couple of beers on tap, while more sophisticated bar-restaurants serve a wider range, including imported New World and European wines. Whisky can be drunk as an aperitif, an after-dinner drink or on its own, and Scotland also serves up an array of speciality beers.

Beer has been brewed in Scotland for more than 2,000 years, and beer drinkers should look out for some unique ales, made to ancient recipes. *Fraoch* ale,

made with heather shoots and flowers, is dark, strong and fragrant. *Grozet* (gooseberry beer) is golden in colour, light and fruity. Ales made with the young shoots of pine and spruce trees were brought to Scotland by the Vikings and remained a Highland favourite until the late 19th century. *Alba* is made to this traditional recipe; with an alcohol content of 7.5 per cent, it makes a pleasant after-dinner drink to be enjoyed at room temperature.

Alcohol-free beverages range from Highland spring water to the uniquely Scottish Irn Bru – a carbonated, caffeinated, artificially flavoured brew. Many Scots swear by it as a hangover cure. Others mix it with vodka.

THE HIGHLAND MENU

Bannocks: oatcakes. Plain biscuits made from oatmeal, usually served with cheese.
Bashit neeps: mashed turnips, usually served as an accompaniment to haggis.
Black pudding: sausage made of blood, fat and offal, served in fried slices for breakfast. Can also be deep fried.
Chappit tatties: mashed potatoes.
Clootie dumpling: sweet, heavy and very filling dessert, similar to Christmas pudding.
Cranachan: dessert made from oatmeal, sweetened cream and fresh berries.
Cullen skink: creamy soup made from smoked fish – similar to chowder.
Fish supper: battered fish (almost always haddock), deep fried and served with chips as a takeaway meal. Known as a 'supper' even when served at lunchtime. If you do not want chips, ask for a 'single fish'.
Haggis: sheep's offal, finely chopped and blended with oatmeal, stuffed into a skin. Usually boiled and served with turnips (neeps) and potatoes (tatties).
Kipper: smoked herring, usually served as a breakfast dish.
Scotch broth: may be made with root vegetables, meat or poultry stock, barley and dried split peas or lentils.
Stovies: stew of meat dripping, potatoes, onions, beef or lamb. Traditionally made with leftover meat scraps from a roast.
Venison: meat of red or roe deer. May be farmed or wild.
White pudding: sausage made from oatmeal, mutton fat, herbs and flavourings. Can be boiled or deep fried.

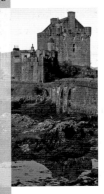

Entertainment

Folk music, homegrown rock and roll, and traditional dance still flourish in the Highlands all year round. However, there are few large entertainment venues, and finding out what is happening – and where – may require some research when you arrive. Local tourist offices usually supply up-to-date listings of events in their region.

Useful sources of information on upcoming shows, concerts, films and events include Scottish newspapers: the *Dundee Courier* and the *Press and Journal* for Grampian, Perthshire and the northeast, the *Inverness Courier* for Inverness and around, the *Oban Times* and *West Highland Free Press* for the west coast, and the *Herald* (published in Glasgow) for the whole region.

Local recreation

Across much of the Scottish Highlands, as in the rest of the UK, the satellite TV, DVD player and computer-game console have supplanted most traditional entertainment – indeed, most Highlanders are more likely to see and hear Scottish performers on-screen than to experience their music live. Watching TV can nevertheless be a communal experience – at least when the widescreen in the pub is showing a major sporting fixture.

The hub of do-it-yourself entertainment in most Highland villages is, however, the village hall, providing a venue for everything from amateur dramatics to wedding receptions, anniversaries, birthday parties and Hogmanay (New Year) celebrations. Any of these events may provide a pretext for a ceilidh. Such nights of music, dancing and drinking are part of a long Highland tradition, and may go on from dusk until dawn. A ceilidh is an informal affair – no invitation is required, but a donation is usually requested to cover the cost of renting the venue and for the hire of a band or sound system. Some venues may have a licence to sell drinks, but in others you might need to bring your own. A ceilidh can be a great night out and a good way to meet local people (and other travellers).

The local live music scene also thrives, with live jazz, folk and rock bands playing in venues ranging from pubs and bars to village halls and city theatres. Legendary bands such as Capercaillie and Runrig and the

Battlefield Band have, over the last 30 years, helped to drive a musical renaissance that fuses Highland and Gaelic roots with rock influences and electronic music, and have inspired a generation of younger musicians. Many of these have made the international big time, but continue to play home-town gigs in Highland venues, and a host of up-and-coming musicians can be discovered locally. Traditional folk-music groups (generically known as 'folkies') often perform in local pubs, many of which advertise regular folk sessions – check the local newspaper for details of these, ask at the local tourist office, or take a look at the noticeboard outside the village hall.

Traditional Highland Games, music and dance

Purists will discover more traditional forms of Highland and Gaelic performing arts at events held by the *Fiesean* movement, which takes its name from the Gaelic word for 'festival'.

Some Highland traditions have survived the commercialisation of entertainment

Festivals and workshops are organised, during which schoolchildren can receive teaching and inspiration in Gaelic song, dance and musical instruments such as the fiddle, *clarsach* (Celtic harp), tin whistle and accordion, from leading performers from around the Celtic fringe. Formal Scottish country dancing is also a popular form of entertainment – for locals as well as visitors to the Highlands – and many larger tourist-oriented hotels host regular performances in summer.

Highland Games held throughout the region offer another chance to see Scottish country dancers performing jigs, reels and strathspeys, and to hear the instrument that visitors associate most strongly with the Highlands: the bagpipes. Pipe music takes many forms. As a spectacle, the sight of a kilted military pipe band in full swing is hard to beat, with massed pipes and drums blasting out the music that has put fear into the hearts of Scotland's enemies for centuries. But there are gentler forms of pipe music, too; the *piobaireachd* or

Sword dancing at the Ballater Highland Games

pibroch can be a moving lament played by a solo piper. These Highland events take place from May to September, but most are held in August. As well as piping and dancing contests and what are known as 'heavy events', in which kilted athletes compete at tossing the caber, throwing the hammer, shot-put and tug-of-war, these displays of tartan pageantry usually also have a range of entertainment for children and can be an excellent day out for families. There are more than 30 Highland Games and gatherings each year and a full, up-to-date list is available on the VisitScotland website: *www.visitscotland.com*

Commercial and mainstream entertainment

Only a few of the larger Highland communities are populous enough to support a cinema and theatre. Exceptions include Fort William, Inverness, Perth, Pitlochry, Thurso and Ullapool. All of these have modern cinemas, which present the latest blockbuster film releases soon after their UK premieres, but Perth and Inverness are the only places with venues that regularly stage major touring theatrical or musical productions. Perth's Concert Hall and Perth Theatre often host performances by leading Scottish dance companies such as Ballet West, as well as concerts of classical and contemporary music by national and international ensembles, as does the Eden Court Theatre in Pitlochry.

The Pitlochry Festival Theatre

The clubbing scene is also somewhat limited, with only Perth and Inverness offering much in the way of DJs and club nights, mainly in small- to medium-sized venues such as Inverness's Ironworks or Alba and the Ice Factory in Perth. However, a number of annual, high-profile open-air summer music and dance festivals – such as RockNess beside Loch Ness, and Loopallu (that's Ullapool spelt backwards) – bring some of the world's top bands, singers and DJs, along with local talent, to venues across the Highlands.

Shopping

The range of things to buy and places to shop in the Highlands is wide, spanning excellent, innovative and expensive artisan-made jewellery, ceramics and textiles and traditional crafts, as well as such internationally renowned products as hand-woven tweed and fine malt whiskies.

Steer clear of shops selling uninspiring mass-produced souvenirs and get a little way off the beaten track; things worth looking out for can include fine handmade silverware, often created by designers who fuse age-old Celtic traditions with modern styles and techniques. Contemporary Highland jewellers also work with semi-precious stones such as amethyst, agate, tourmaline, garnet and rose quartz, though these days the stones themselves are more likely to have been imported from Brazil or Asia than to have been found locally. There are also numerous pottery and ceramics workshops dotted around the Highlands, some of which turn out beautifully designed and produced work, while others are less creative. Woollen knitwear can also be a good buy, and the visitor will often find an immediate use for a new sweater or cardigan in Scotland's cool climate. Sheepskin coats, jackets and slippers can be worth investing in, too. The

Inveraray Woollen Mill (*Front Street, Inveraray. Tel: (01499) 302 166. www.inverarraywoollenmill.com*) offers one-stop shopping for woollens, tweeds and whiskies. Malt whisky connoisseurs will also find a huge selection of malts and blends sold at the many distilleries on Speyside, including cask-strength malts and exciting new styles of whisky that are hard to find outside Scotland.

Most Highland town centres, as well as villages on the well-trodden tourist trails, also have more than their fair share of antique shops, but it has to be said that Scotland has been systematically pillaged by antique and antiquarian dealers for decades. Most antiques and curios are seriously overpriced, and the visitor's chances of finding a rare and exciting bargain are exceedingly small.

Visitors can also find numerous farm and fishery shops selling a wide range of local produce, much of which is raised organically. The **Loch Fyne**

Oyster Company (*Clachan, Cairndow. Tel: (01499) 600 264. www.lochfyne.com*) sells marvellous smoked salmon and smoked oysters, as well as an array of fresh seafood, venison and organically raised beef and lamb, which it can have delivered to your home in the UK or abroad.

Visitors who want to boast of their Scottish ancestry can find kiltmakers in places like Inverness, Perth and Oban, selling made-to-measure and off-the-peg kilt outfits in every imaginable tartan – indeed, some will even create new custom-made tartans for clients who cannot find a plaid to suit them. For a full kilt outfit, comprising a handmade kilt, hose, shoes, jacket and other accessories, the price can be as high as £900.

Hector Russell (*6–8 Bridge Street, Inverness. Tel: 0800 980 4010. www.hector-russell.com*) is one of Scotland's leading kiltmakers, with retail outlets also in Oban, Fort William and Pitlochry.

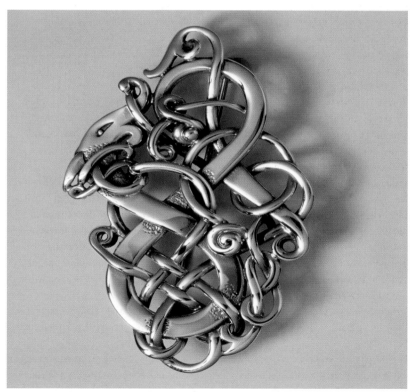

A silver brooch based on Celtic intertwining knots

Sport and leisure

Highland Scotland is above all an outdoor destination, with plenty of land- and water-based activities on offer. On land, there is mountain biking, hillwalking, rock climbing, quad biking and 4WD safaris. On water, there's white-water rafting and canoeing on Highland rivers, sea kayaking around offshore isles, surfing on northern beaches, yacht and dinghy sailing on lochs and sea lochs, as well as angling and scuba diving.

All of these land and sea activities are as popular with Scots as with visitors. The best resource for finding organised adventure specialists and where to hire equipment throughout the Highlands is **VisitScotland** (*Tel: (0845) 225 5121. www.visitscotland.com/adventure*).

Almost all of the Highlands, including privately owned land, is by law freely accessible for activities including walking, cycling, riding, canoeing and wild camping. However, these access rights do not apply to motorised vehicles of any kind, or to activities such as shooting, hunting and fishing. **Scottish National Heritage** (*Tel: (01738) 444 177. www.outdooraccess-scotland.com*) publishes the Scottish Outdoor Access Code, which outlines rights and responsibilities.

Cycling

The Highlands offer great terrain for on- and off-road cycling, with numerous challenging, purpose-built mountain-bike circuits and forest trails.

Away from major highways, country roads generally do not carry heavy motor vehicle traffic. VisitScotland publishes the *Scottish Mountain Biking Guide*, which lists more than 20 off-road trails, rated from green (for novice riders) to black (for expert mountain cyclists), as well as details of cyclist-friendly places to stay and equipment providers. The Cyclists Welcome Scheme features several hundred places to stay that offer services specially for cyclists, including lockable bike storage, a hot drink on arrival, late evening meals and early breakfasts, clothes-drying facilities, and information on local cycle runs and public transport.

Football

Football (which is never called 'soccer') is a national obsession in Scotland, but the Highlands have only one Premier League team, Inverness Caledonian Thistle FC. For tickets and fixtures, *see www.ictfc.co.uk*. Less illustrious teams compete in the **Highland Football**

League (*www.highlandfootballleague.com*) but only a few – Fort William FC, Clachnacuddin FC (Inverness), Brora Rovers and Wick Academy – have their home in the Highlands proper. The season extends from early August to mid-May, and most matches are held on Saturday afternoons. It's worth noting that when major matches are scheduled, the sale of alcohol may be banned on some Scottish trains to reduce football-related hooliganism.

Golf

Scotland is the birthplace of golf, and although most of its high-profile courses are in the Lowlands, several renowned golf courses can be found in the north, notably at Dunkeld, Loch Lomond and Dornoch (*see Directory chapter for details of clubs and access*).

Highland Games and native Highland sports

If there is one sporting event that is most closely associated with the Highlands, it must be tossing the caber, which, along with putting the stone, throwing the hammer, and the team tug-o'-war, is one of the key 'heavy events' that form the sporting centrepiece of dozens of Highland Games around the country from May until September. Although it is often claimed that these events originated in ancient times, during the heyday of the clans, when they were used as tests of warrior prowess, they are in truth a much more recent development, popularised during the 19th century when Queen Victoria and her entourage became romantically obsessed with all things tartan.

A funicular runs up to the Cairn Gorm Mountain ski area

Authentic or not, Highland Games are still great fun. A full calendar of each year's events, with details of venues and where to buy tickets, can be found on the VisitScotland website.

Other native Highland sports include shinty or *camanachd*, which has been played here for some 1,500 years. Very similar to the Irish game of hurling, it features teams of 12 players equipped with curved wooden sticks (called *camans*), whose objective is to whack a small hard ball into the opposing team's goal. Unlike in hockey, sticks may be raised above shoulder level and the ball may be played in the air. In short, it's a fast and furious game and very exciting to watch. The season runs from March to October and

details of upcoming fixtures and where to buy tickets can be obtained from the **Camanachd Association** (*Tel: (01463) 715 931. www.shinty.com*).

Hiking and walking

Few activities lend themselves so well to the breathtaking Highland landscape as hiking and hillwalking. To enhance your experience and save time, opt for a guided walking holiday. Walking companies will arrange for your luggage to be transported ahead of you as you walk, provide local transport and the services of an expert guide, and arrange accommodation in tents, hostels or upmarket hotels. Most also have eco-sensitive travel policies in place and work actively to preserve

The Loch Morlich Watersports Centre at Glenmore, by Aviemore

Scotland's beautiful landscapes – and a guided walking trip is also a great way to meet Scots, who are keen walkers in their own country. Most tours are in groups of from 6 to 12 walkers.

VisitScotland, with the **Forestry Commission** (*Tel: (0845) 367 3787*), publishes an annually updated guide, *Walk in Scotland*, listing dozens of self-guided walks and walker-friendly places to stay. Other useful contacts for walkers and climbers include the **Mountaineering Council of Scotland** (*Tel: (01738) 638 227. www.mcofs.org.uk*), which provides detailed information on environmental issues and access.

Water-, winter and other sports

For experienced scuba divers, Scotland offers some outstanding underwater experiences, especially on the west coast, where there are a number of dives on wrecks, walls and underwater pinnacles, and in huge 'kelp forests', with remarkable sea life. Dry-suit skills are required even for summer diving. For details of certified dive centres, contact the **British Sub Aqua Club** (*www.bsac.org*).

VisitScotland produces brochures devoted to riding and pony trekking in the Highlands and operates a website (*www.sailscotland.co.uk*) for yacht and dinghy sailors, with details of harbours, marinas, sailing schools and boat rental and charter operators.

Winter sports are available at Glenshee, Aviemore, and the Lecht in the Grampian Highlands, and at the Nevis Range and Glencoe near Fort William. Stations are well equipped and accessible, and equipment can be rented and although snow conditions are unreliable, in a 'good' year skiing may be possible from December until Easter.

Another home-grown game, curling, is popular all over Scotland (and in Canada, to where it has been exported by Highland emigrants). The game dates from the 16th century, and originally involved sliding massive 'stones' of polished granite (weighing some 18kg/40lb) across a frozen pond to a central target. Now, owing to global warming, few Scottish lakes and ponds freeze solid every winter, and it is more usually played on indoor ice rinks. Details of fixtures and venues can be found on the website of the sport's organising association, the **Royal Caledonian Curling Club** (*www. royalcaledoniancurlingclub.org*).

Safety information

For all sports, safety standards are generally high, with equipment suppliers and outdoor adventure companies providing adequate safety equipment and advice. Ironically, 'gentler' activities such as hillwalking cause more fatalities each year than 'extreme' sports, simply because inexperienced and ill-equipped walkers are too often ignorant of the risks of fast-changing weather and rough terrain and set out on demanding walks without expert guidance.

Children

Highland Scotland is one of the world's best destinations for active families, with a huge choice of activities, sights and attractions that appeal to all ages. Children brought up in a city environment will be wowed by wide, open spaces and long, empty beaches. The region also has a plethora of all-weather attractions such as wildlife parks, leisure centres with pools, interactive museums and visitor centres.

As in the rest of the UK, most restaurants are willing to cater for children, and some offer typical children's menus. Children are generally less welcome in bars and pubs, except for those that seek to attract families with outdoor areas for children and family menus.

Most visitor attractions welcome children and offer a child discount, usually around 50 per cent for children under 12. Parents with younger children should be aware that many historical attractions – ruined castles and the like – do not always have easy access for pushchairs and can be difficult for toddlers to negotiate, with steep stairs and sometimes scary-looking heights to contend with. Specialist tour operators in many places offer packages specially designed for families, with adventure activities such as mountain biking, river rafting and canoeing. Standards of safety and equipment are generally high. In terms of accommodation, Highland

Scotland's big network of youth hostels offers excellent value for families, with en-suite family rooms sleeping six to eight children and adults in single beds and bunks. Most guesthouses and hotels can provide child beds with sufficient advance notice, and many allow children under ten to share a room with parents at no extra cost.

Wildlife watching has great appeal for many children, and the wild is nowhere closer than in the Highlands. Just 5km (3 miles) north of Inverness, children can watch rare red kites on their nests using closed-circuit TV, or go on a seal- and dolphin-spotting cruise from the **North Kessock Dolphin and Seal Centre** (*see p111*). The Royal Zoological Society of Scotland's **Highland Wildlife Park**, near Kingussie (*Tel: (01540) 651 270. www.highlandwildlifepark.org*), is an open-air zoo with a collection of animals and birds on view that still live wild in the Highlands, as well as wolves, beaver, lynx and bison, animals that once lived here and are now extinct, but which may one day be reintroduced.

Museums with special appeal for children include the **Highland Museum of Childhood** in Strathpeffer (*Tel: (01997) 421 031. www. highlandmuseumofchildhood.org.uk*), which focuses on childhood in the Highlands in times gone by, with a collection of toys, dolls and games. In Kingussie and Newtonmore, the **Highland Folk Museum** (*Tel: (01540) 673 551. www.highlandfolk.com*) is an open-air museum with lots of activities in summer and exhibits including a traditional 'black house', farming and weaving equipment, costumes, musical instruments, traditional furniture and a special exhibition on the lifestyle and history of Highland travelling people. **Inveraray Jail** (*Tel: (01499) 302 381. www.inverarayjail.co.uk*), with its actor-guides playing the roles of 19th-century warders and prisoners, is perhaps a bit too scary for littler children, but great for older kids, and the *In Prison Today* section, looking at life behind bars in the 21st century, may help to keep them on the straight and narrow.

A wolf on the prowl at the Highland Wildlife Park

Essentials

Arriving and departing
By air
Inverness Airport (*www.hial.co.uk/ inverness-airport*), 10km (6 miles) from the city, is the only major airport within the Highlands region. Main carriers include **easyJet** (*www.easyjet.com*) with flights from London Gatwick, Luton and Bristol; **Ryanair** (*www.ryanair.com*) from East Midlands; and **British Midland** (*www.bmibaby.com*) from London Heathrow. The only international connection to Inverness is from Düsseldorf with **Lufthansa** (*www. lufthansa.com*). Otherwise, **Glasgow International** (*www.glasgowairport.com*) and **Edinburgh International** (*www. edinburghairport.com*) are served by flights from most European capitals, the US and Canada. Both of these are around one hour's drive from the southern fringes of the Highlands. All major car-rental services have desks at both of these airports.

By rail
Rail services from London to Inverness via Perth are operated on the east coast route by **East Coast** (*www.eastcoast.co.uk*) and on the west coast route by **Virgin Trains** (*www.virgintrains.co.uk*). Fastest journey time is around six hours to Perth and eight hours to Inverness; however, neither company operates more than one direct service daily.

Some services require two or three changes of train and can take up to 14 hours to Inverness from London. **First ScotRail** (*Tel: (0845) 55 00 33. www.scotrail.co.uk*) operates overnight Caledonian Sleeper services from London to Inverness via Perth and from London to Fort William.

By road
The M1/A1 east coast motorway connects London and southeast England with Edinburgh, from where the M90 motorway takes you to Perth. From Perth, the A9 highway leads north to Inverness, then up the northeast coast to Thurso.

The M6/A74/M74 route connects southern England with Glasgow, from where the A82 leads north to Fort William, then northeast to Inverness. Driving time to Glasgow or Edinburgh from London is around eight hours.

Frequent long-distance bus services operate from London and other major British cities to Glasgow and Edinburgh, with connections from these cities to the main Highland towns. The main coach operators are **National Express** (*Tel: 08717 81 81 78. www.nationalexpress.com*), **Citylink** (*Tel: (0871) 266 3333. www.citylink.co. uk*) and **Megabus** (*Tel: (0900) 160 1900. www.megabus.com*). The coach journey from London to Edinburgh or Glasgow takes 10–11 hours.

By sea

DFDS Seaways (*Tel: (0871) 574 7300.
www.dfdsseaways.co.uk*) operates the
only international ferry service to
Scotland, carrying cars and foot
passengers from Zeebrugge in Belgium
to Rosyth, 48km (30 miles) south of
Perth. The crossing takes about
20 hours.

Customs and immigration

There are no customs and immigration
formalities on entering Scotland from
England as both are part of the United
Kingdom. Visitors arriving by air must
clear Customs at their arrival airport.
Visitors arriving by sea (via the
Zeebrugge–Rosyth crossing) clear
Customs at Rosyth. Those arriving
from the EU may bring in unlimited
goods for personal use. Those arriving
from non-EU countries may bring in
one litre of spirits plus two litres of still
wine, 200 cigarettes or 50 cigars, 500cc
of perfume, and gifts up to a value of
£150 duty free.

Electricity

Scotland uses the same 240 AC system
and three-pin sockets as the rest of the
UK. Visitors from outside the UK will
require an adaptor.

Internet

Internet access is widely available, with
numerous Internet centres in main
towns. In smaller places, visitors may be
able to get online in the local library or
community centre. Most hotels of

A steam train on the West Highland Line

three-star standard and above have
Internet access either in rooms or in
public areas, and many now have Wi-Fi
access for an additional charge.
There are also numerous Wi-Fi
hotspots strategically located in larger
towns. In practice, Wi-Fi access tends to
be overpriced in hotels and at railway
stations and airports, but many bars
and cafés offer free access to patrons.

Money

Scotland uses the British pound
(sterling), divided into 100 pence.
Coins are in denominations of 1p,
2p, 5p, 10p, 20p, 50p, £1 and £2. Notes
are in £5, £10, £20, £50 and £100
denominations. Confusingly for the

visitor, three main Scottish banks – the Clydesdale Bank, Bank of Scotland and Royal Bank of Scotland – issue their own sterling notes, which are equally acceptable everywhere in Scotland along with Bank of England currency. However, it is worth exchanging any leftover Scottish currency for English notes before leaving Scotland at the end of your holiday – Scottish banknotes are hard to exchange outside the UK and may sometimes be refused, even in England.

Major international credit cards, charge cards and debit cards using the Cirrus/Maestro system are acceptable almost everywhere, although the smallest family-run B&Bs may prefer to be paid in cash. All major currencies and traveller's cheques can be exchanged at banks throughout the Highlands, and

Memorial to the massacre of Glencoe

ATMs in all but the smallest villages accept most credit and debit cards. Banks are normally open from Monday to Friday, 9.30am–3.30pm.

Opening hours

In major towns such as Perth and Inverness, shops normally open from Monday to Saturday between 9am and 6pm. Many close for lunch between 12.30pm and 1.30pm and some close on Saturday afternoon. Larger supermarkets open from Monday to Saturday, 9am–6pm, and are usually open 10am–6pm on Sundays.

Bars and restaurants serving alcohol normally open at noon (sometimes at 11am) and stay open until 11pm or midnight; at weekends, some bars, especially those with live music, stay open as late as 1am. Clubs may stay open until 2am.

Passports and visas

A valid passport is required for all visitors. No visa is required for citizens of EU countries, who may stay in the UK indefinitely. US, Canadian, Australian and New Zealand citizens do not require a visa for stays of up to six months, but may have to show evidence of sufficient funds and/or a return ticket.

Pharmacies

All towns have several pharmacies (chemists) and most larger villages have at least one. Chemists are open during normal shopping hours, but a rota ensures that at least one chemist in each area stays open on Sundays.

Post

Post offices can be found in the centre of all major towns. In smaller villages, sub-post offices operate out of local shops and offer all the postal services normally required by visitors, including sale of stamps. Stamps can also be bought from vending machines at post offices and are sold in most newsagents and local shops. Postboxes are red.

Public holidays

New Year: 1–2 Jan
Easter: Mar/Apr variable
Early May Bank Holiday:
First Monday in May
Spring Bank Holiday:
Last Monday in May
Summer Bank Holiday:
First Monday in Aug
St Andrew's Day: 30 Nov
Christmas Day: 25 Dec
Boxing Day: 26 Dec
If Christmas Day or Boxing Day falls on a Saturday or Sunday, the next weekday becomes a public holiday.

Smoking

Smoking is prohibited on public transport and in all indoor public spaces, including bars, pubs, offices, restaurants, shops, hotel public areas, railway stations, bus stations and airports. Hotels may at their own discretion offer bedrooms designated for smokers.

Suggested reading and media

Glencoe (1961), *Culloden* (1961) and *The Highland Clearances* (1963) by John Prebble, all published by Penguin, are highly readable accounts of three traumatic events in Highlands history. Prebble is also the author of *The Lion in the North* (Penguin, 1971), an equally readable overview of Highlands and Scottish history. *Kidnapped* (1886, various publishers) by Robert Louis Stevenson, set in the Highlands in the aftermath of the '45 rising, is possibly the best Scottish historical novel ever written. *I Never Knew That About Scotland* (Ebury Press, 2007) by Christopher Winn is a delightful compendium of Scottish trivia which is guaranteed to keep any Highlands traveller amused for hours. *Scotland the Best* (Collins, updated annually) by Peter Irvine is an indispensable and comprehensive traveller's companion, listing everything from the best walks and views to the best surf beaches, picnic spots, attractions for children and places to see whales and dolphins.

Newspapers covering the regions featured in this book include the *Dundee Courier* and the *Press and Journal* (Perthshire, Grampian and the northeast), the *Inverness Courier* (Inverness and around), the *Oban Times* and *West Highland Free Press* (the west coast), and the *Herald* (published in Glasgow), which covers the whole region.

Scotland receives the main UK terrestrial TV channels BBC1, BBC2,

Channels 4 and Five, together with BBC Scotland, which produces its own news, current affairs, documentary and drama programmes for a Scottish audience. The ITV1 franchises, STV and Grampian, between them cover most of the west and northeast. Most homes and most hotels and guesthouses also subscribe to the usual global array of satellite channels. BBC Radio's five main channels, plus the homegrown **BBC Radio Scotland**, cover the entire region, along with numerous regionally based stations, including the UK's smallest, **Lochbroom FM. BBC Radio nan Gaidheal** broadcasts in Gaelic and plays some of the best traditional and contemporary Celtic music. Radio Scotland's regular traffic and weather updates (every 30 mins) are invaluable for drivers and walkers.

BBC Radio Scotland 92–95FM, 810MW.
www.bbc.co.uk/radioscotland
Lochbroom FM 102.2FM and 96.8FM.
www.lochbroomfm.co.uk
BBC Radio nan Gaidheal 103.4FM.
www.bbc.co.uk/scotland/alba

Sustainable tourism

Thomas Cook is a strong advocate of ethical and fairly traded tourism and believes that the travel experience

A late sunset over the pier at Rowardennan, Loch Lomond

should be as good for the places visited as it is for the people who visit them. That's why we firmly support The Travel Foundation, a charity that develops solutions to help improve and protect holiday destinations, their environment, traditions and culture. To find out what you can do to make a positive difference to the places you travel to and the people who live there, please visit *www.makeholidaysgreener.org.uk*

Taxes and tipping

Value Added Tax (VAT) at 20 per cent is levied on most goods and services. There are no local sales taxes. Visitors from outside the EU can reclaim VAT on major purchases on leaving the UK. A tip of 10 per cent is adequate in restaurants and hotels.

Telephones

Public payphones can be found at most railway stations and coach stations and in many pubs, bars and restaurants and in hotel lobbies. Some smaller guesthouses and B&Bs also have payphones. Coin-operated payphones take 10p, 20p, 50p and £1 and phones also accept credit and debit cards. Mobile phone coverage is extensive, but finding a signal in some remoter glens can be difficult. Mobile phones in Scotland use the GSM system; some mobile phones bought in the US and Canada will not work in the UK. Numbers with the prefix *0800* are toll-free. Many information and

reservation lines use *0845* or *0870*. These are non-geographic numbers for which a range of premium rates are charged.

Time

Scotland is on Greenwich Mean Time (GMT), with one hour added in summer (late March to late October). From early November to late March, when it is noon in Scotland it is 1pm in Paris, 3pm in Moscow, 11pm in Sydney and 7am in New York and Toronto.

Toilets

Public toilets are located at railway and bus stations, and in shopping centres and main streets of larger towns. Most are automated, with wheelchair access. There is usually a small charge. All licensed restaurants, pubs and bars have toilets for the use of patrons; standards of cleanliness vary, and not all establishments are accessible to wheelchairs. Cafés and tearooms that do not serve alcohol are not required to provide toilets.

Travellers with disabilities

There is adequate wheelchair access at most major visitor attractions operated by organisations such as Historic Scotland and the National Trust for Scotland, at most museums and most privately run visitor attractions. Many sights also have induction-loop audio guides for people with impaired hearing, and audio guides for partially sighted people.

Emergencies

Emergencies
Police, Fire, Ambulance *999*

Medical services
Major hospitals with accident and emergency services include:

Perthshire Highlands
Perth Royal Infirmary
Taymount Terrace, Perth.
Tel: (01738) 623 311.

Highland Argyll
Belford Hospital
Fort William. Tel: (01397) 702 481.

Inverness and around
Raigmore Hospital
Old Perth Road, Inverness.
Tel: (01463) 704 000.

Northeast Highlands
Caithness General Hospital
Barklands Road, Wick.
Tel: (01955) 605 050.

For all other medical and emergency needs, consult
www.nhshighland.scot.nhs.uk

Opticians
Opticians providing a full range of services, including contact lenses, frame repair and replacement lenses, can be found in main towns in the Highlands including Perth, Inverness, Ullapool, Oban, Fort William, Wick and Thurso.

Health and accident insurance
This is strongly recommended, especially for visitors planning outdoor activity holidays such as hillwalking, kayaking, sailing and climbing. Visitors who intend to pursue such sports as deer stalking, grouse shooting and salmon fishing, which require specialist equipment and involve special risks (such as being shot at accidentally by other sportspeople), should seek the advice of a specialist insurer.

Pay attention to the signs when hiking in the Highlands

Health risks

No major health risks. Tiny, biting flies called midges can be a pest in parts of the Highlands, especially the northwest and northeast, from May to September, but are not disease-carrying. They are not deterred by mosquito deterrent, but can be kept off by applying a layer of baby oil or the moisturiser Skin-So-Soft (made by Avon) to exposed skin.

Safety and crime

Despite the region's idyllic reputation, Highland Scotland has, like many parts of the UK, issues with drug and alcohol abuse, and crime. Theft from (and of) vehicles is not uncommon. Do not leave valuables where they can be seen in parked vehicles. Town centres may also have the same problems with late-night revellers as their English counterparts, when the pubs and clubs close. On public transport, keep a close eye on your possessions.

Crimes in progress should be reported by dialling 999; after the event, go to the nearest police station, where you will be given a crime report statement for insurance purposes.

Embassies

There are no embassies in the region – London addresses are listed below:

Australia

Australian High Commission
Australia House, Strand
Charing Cross

London WC2B 4LA.
Tel: (020) 7379 4334.
www.uk.embassy.gov.au

Canada

Canadian High Commission
1 Grosvenor Square
London W1K 4AB.
Tel: (020) 7258 6600.
www.canada.org.uk

Ireland

Irish Embassy
17 Grosvenor Place
London SW1X 7HR.
Tel: (020) 7235 2171.
http://ireland.embassyhomepage.com

New Zealand

New Zealand High Commission
New Zealand House
80 Haymarket
London SW1Y 4TQ.
Tel: (020) 7930 8422.
www.nzembassy.com/uk

South Africa

South African High Commission
South Africa House
Trafalgar Square
London WC2N 5DP.
Tel: (020) 7451 7299.
www.southafricahouse.com

US

US Embassy, 24 Grosvenor Square
London W1A 2LQ.
Tel: (020) 7499 9000.
www.usembassy.org.uk

Directory

Price guide

In this directory, prices for accommodation and places to eat are graded on a scale of one to four stars. Please note that these bear no relation to VisitScotland's rating system. Accommodation prices are based on the average price of a double room. Eating out prices are based on the average cost of a three-course meal for one person, not including drinks.

Accommodation price guide

| ★ | Less than £50 | ★★★ | £80–£150 |
| ★★ | £50–£80 | ★★★★ | More than £150 |

Eating out price guide

| ★ | Less than £15 | ★★★ | £25–£50 |
| ★★ | £15–£25 | ★★★★ | More than £50 |

PERTHSHIRE HIGHLANDS
Aberfeldy
ACCOMMODATION
Fortingall Hotel ★★★
Attractive and comfortable hotel close to Loch Tay, in a thatched, white-painted 17th-century building, with its own highly acclaimed restaurant. *Fortingall, Aberfeldy. Tel: (01887) 830 367. www.fortingall.com*
Kenmore Hotel ★★★
Very attractive old inn, newly refurbished, which claims to be the oldest inn in Scotland. *The Square, Kenmore, A827, 8km (5 miles) west of Aberfeldy. Tel: (01887) 830 205. www.kenmorehotel.com*

EATING OUT
Aberfeldy Weem Hotel ★★
With locally produced ingredients such as shellfish from Loch Fyne, Scottish beef and hill lamb, this inn is by far the best place to eat in the Aberfeldy area. *Weem, Aberfeldy. Tel: (01887) 820 381. www.weemhotel.com*

SPORT AND LEISURE
Ace Adventures
Activities include birdwatching, walking, river safaris, cycle tours, canyoning, canoeing, white-water rafting and mountain-bike hire. *Grampian Road, Aviemore. Tel: (03305) 550 313. www.aceadventures.co.uk*
Highland Safaris
4WD adventures and wildlife walks in a

158

101,200-hectare (250,000-acre) private estate near Aberfeldy.
Aberfeldy.
Tel: (01887) 820 071.
www.highlandsafaris.net

Dunkeld

ACCOMMODATION
Hilton Dunkeld House ★★★★
Set in 113.3 hectares (280 acres) of grounds beside the Tay, this fine hotel was once the mansion of the dukes of Atholl. Its leisure complex provides a range of activities such as quad riding and clay shooting, and there is an 18-hole golf course 800m (½ mile) from the hotel.
Dunkeld.
Tel: (01350) 727 771.
www.hilton.co.uk/ dunkeld

EATING OUT
The Darjeeling ★
Affordable Indian restaurant offering good-quality South Asian cooking and a reasonable choice of vegetarian dishes.
Main Street, Dunkeld.
Tel: (01350) 727 427.

ENTERTAINMENT
The Taybank
This pub is a long-standing magnet for Scottish musicians, with regular gigs.
Tay Terrace, Dunkeld.
Tel: (01350) 727 340.
www.thetaybank.com

SPORT AND LEISURE
Dunkeld and Birnam Golf Club
This fine heathland course, founded more than 100 years ago, was extended to 18 holes in 2000.
Fungarth, Dunkeld.
Tel: (01350) 727 524.
www.dunkeldandbirnam golfclub.co.uk

Perth

ACCOMMODATION
New County Hotel ★★
Traditional hotel with 23 bedrooms, café, bar and à la carte brasserie restaurant in the centre of Perth; extensively restored and upgraded in 2001.
22–30 County Place, Perth.
Tel: (01783) 623 355.
www.newcountyhotel.com

EATING OUT
Glassrooms ★★
Pleasant, modern café-bar and digital art space

within the Perth Concert Hall.
Perth Concert Hall, 187 High Street, Perth.
Tel: (01738) 477 724.
www.horsecross.co.uk
Deans@Let's Eat ★★★
The best restaurant in Perth and one of the best in Scotland.
77–79 Kinnoull Street, Perth.
Tel: (01738) 643 377.
www.letseatperth.co.uk

ENTERTAINMENT
Loft Nightclub
Perth's most sophisticated nightspot boasts three bars (including an upper-level cocktail lounge) and a playlist that includes party classics and the latest dance tracks. It also has its own stretch limo. Fridays and Saturdays are over-21 nights.
145–149 South Street, Perth.
Tel: (01783) 634 523.
www.loftclub.co.uk
Perth Concert Hall and Theatre
The region's premier entertainment venue hosts theatre, ballet, dance and live performances from musicians ranging from

Deacon Blue to the Scottish Fiddle Orchestra and the National Youth Orchestra of Scotland.
187 High Street, Perth.
Tel: (01738) 621 031.
www.horsecross.co.uk
Festival:
www.perthfestival.co.uk

SPORT AND LEISURE
Perth Leisure Pool
Swimming and leisure centre with six pools (including a heated, all-weather outdoor lagoon), flumes and spa.
Glasgow Road, Perth.
Tel: (01738) 492 421.
www.liveactive.co.uk

Perth Races
Scotland's premier race-course attracts some of Britain's leading owners, jockeys and spectators.
Scone Palace Park, Perth.
Tel: (01738) 551 597.
www.perth-races.co.uk

Pitlochry
ACCOMMODATION
Pitlochry Youth Hostel ★
Four-bed family rooms are available here, as well as dormitory bunks.
Knockard Road, Pitlochry.
Tel: (01796) 472 308.
www.syha.org.uk

Craigatin House ★★
Affordable and stylish guesthouse, with 'boutique hotel' aspirations.
165 Atholl Road, Pitlochry.
Tel: (01796) 472 478.
www.craigatinhouse.co.uk

Killiecrankie Hotel ★★★
Small hotel with ten rooms and two good restaurants.
Killiecrankie, B8079 off the A9, 5km (3 miles) north of Pitlochry.
Tel: (01796) 473 220.
www.killiecrankiehotel.co.uk

Scotland's Hotel and Leisure Club ★★★
Housed in a Victorian mock-baronial building, this hotel offers affordable luxury, modern amenities and leisure facilities.
40 Bonnethill Road, Pitlochry.
Tel: (0870) 950 6282.
www.crerarhotels.com

EATING OUT
Strathgarry Café & Bar ★
Serving breakfast, morning coffee, lunch, afternoon tea and pre-theatre dinners (reservation recommended).

Strathgarry Hotel,
113 Atholl Road, Pitlochry.
Tel: (01796) 472 469. www.strathgarryhotel.co.uk.
Open: all day.

Port na Craig ★★
Pleasant brasserie-style restaurant on the south bank of the River Tay.
Port na Craig Road, Pitlochry.
Tel: (01796) 472 777.
www.portnacraig.com

ENTERTAINMENT
Pitlochry Festival Theatre
One of Scotland's best contemporary repertory theatres. Reservation almost always needed.
Port na Craig, Pitlochry.
Tel: (01796) 484 626.
www.pitlochry.org.co.uk.
Open: all year.

SPORT AND LEISURE
Nae Limits
Innovative activity company offering family rafting, paintball, canyoning, clay shooting, sphereing, quad bikes and more.
Ballinluig, off the A9 southbound, 8km (5 miles) south of Pitlochry.
Tel: (0845) 017 8177.
www.naelimits.co.uk

GRAMPIAN HIGHLANDS AND CAIRNGORMS

Aviemore

ACCOMMODATION

Aviemore Youth Hostel ★
Purpose-built hostel in a modern building five minutes from the town centre, with family rooms and en-suite private rooms as well as dorm bunks.
25 Grampian Road, Aviemore.
Tel: (01479) 810 345.
www.syha.org.uk. Open: all year.

Cairngorm Lodge ★
Comfortable hostel in the heart of Cairngorms National Park. Above-average facilities include conservatory restaurant.
Glenmore, B970, 8km (5 miles) south of Aviemore.
Tel: (01479) 861 238.
www.syha.org.uk.
Closed: 25 Oct–20 Dec.

Macdonald Aviemore Highland Resort Hotel ★★★★
Four hotels, including one luxury hotel, share the same grounds and a range of facilities, including six restaurants and the Macdonald Aviemore Highland Leisure Arena.
Macdonald Aviemore Highland Resort, Grampian Road, Aviemore.
Tel: (0844) 879 9152.
www.aviemorehighland resort.co.uk

EATING OUT

Old Bridge Inn ★
Great char grilled steaks, cask ales and a good selection of malt whiskies.
Dalfaber Road, Aviemore.
Tel: (01479) 811 137.
www.oldbridgeinn.co.uk

Harkai's Happy Haggis ★★
Long-established Aviemore favourite.
45 Grampian Road, Aviemore.
Tel: (01479) 810 430.
www.harkai.co.uk. Closed: two weeks in May; Nov.

ENTERTAINMENT

Cairngorm Hotel Bar
Always lively with nightly entertainment. Quiz nights on Tuesdays, karaoke on Sundays.
15 Grampian Road, Aviemore.
Tel: (01479) 810 233.
www.cairngorm.com

SPORT AND LEISURE

Ace Adventures
Offers outdoor activities including birdwatching, walking, river safaris, family bike tours, canyoning, canoeing, white-water rafting and mountain-bike hire.
Grampian Road, Aviemore.
Tel: (01479) 810 510.
www.aceadventures.co.uk

G2 Outdoor
Skiing and other winter sports, mini-rafting, gorge walking and winter skills training.
Unit 3, Plot 10, Dalfaber Industrial Estate, Aviemore.
Tel: (01497) 811 008.
www.g2outdoor.co.uk

Outdoor Discovery
Outstanding activity centre with dry ski slope, bike hire, skate park, climbing walls and 'super-jumper' trampoline.
Coylumbridge, Aviemore.
Tel: (01479) 811 066. www. outdoordiscovery.co.uk

Ballater & Braemar

ACCOMMODATION

Braemar Youth Hostel ★
Comfortable hostel in old shooting lodge on outskirts of Braemar offers the cheapest accommodation in town.

Family rooms and private rooms available, as well as bunk-bedded dorms.
Corrie Feragie, 21 Glenshee Road, Braemar. Tel: (01399) 741 659. www.syha.org.uk. Closed: 31 Oct–4 Jan.

The Auld Kirk ★★

Delightful small restaurant with rooms (just six of them, all en-suite and all beautifully presented).
Braemar Road, Ballater. Tel: (01339) 755 672. www.theauldkirk.com

Darroch Learg ★★★

Extremely pleasant mansion-house hotel on the outskirts of town with the best restaurant in Ballater (open to non-residents).
Darroch Brae, Ballater. Tel: (01339) 755 443. www.darrochlearg.co.uk

EATING OUT

The Spirit Restaurant ★★★

Fine dining and an excellent wine list, with a menu that emphasises local produce.
The Auld Kirk, Braemar Road, Ballater. Tel: (01339) 755 672. www.theauldkirk.com

SPORT AND LEISURE

Glenshee Ski Centre

The UK's largest ski centre with 36 runs and 21 lifts and tows, also popular with snowboarders. Dry ski slope available.
Cairnwell, 15km (9 miles) south of Braemar. Tel: (01339) 741 320. www.ski-glenshee.co.uk

Kingussie & Newtonmore

ACCOMMODATION

Glenfeshie Hostel ★

Bunkhouse accommodation for up to 16 people in the heart of the Cairngorms National Park; three bunk rooms, one room with four single beds, communal cooking area, laundry and drying room.
Kincraig, Feshiebridge. Tel: (01540) 651 323. www.glenfeshiehostel.co.uk

EATING OUT

The Cross ★★★

This outstanding restaurant has a pretty location and also has attractive bedrooms for those wishing to stay the night. Reservation essential.
Tweed Mill Brae, Ardbroilach Road. Tel: (01540) 661 166. www.thecross.co.uk

ENTERTAINMENT

Waltzing Waters

Fantastic and colourful water, light and music production.
Balavil Brae, Newtonmore. Tel: (01540) 673 752. www.waltzingwaters.co.uk

SPORT AND LEISURE

See Aviemore (p161) for sport and leisure activities in the Kingussie & Newtonmore area.

HIGHLAND ARGYLL

Fort William

ACCOMMODATION

Clachaig Inn ★/★★

Comfortable 23-bedroom inn with three lively bars, in a perfect location for exploring Glencoe on foot. Good solid pub grub (including a better than average menu for vegetarians), and great atmosphere. All rooms are en-suite; not all have bathtubs. Self-catering accommodation also available.

Old Glencoe Village Road, Glencoe.
Tel: (01855) 811 252.
www.clachaig.com

Glencoe Hotel ★★

This attractive little inn with 15 rooms overlooks Loch Leven at the foot of Glenshee and has recently been refurbished to a comfortably high standard. Fort William is only 20 minutes away.

Glencoe Village, Glencoe.
Tel: (01855) 811 245.
www.crerarhotels.com

The Grange ★★

Fort William's best B&B. Fabulous views over the loch from all four en-suite rooms.

Grange Road, Fort William.
Tel: (01397) 705 516.
www.thegrange-scotland.co.uk

Lime Tree Studios ★★

Fort William's trendiest place to stay, with nine en-suite rooms above an excellent restaurant-cum-art gallery.

Cameron Square,
Achintore Road,
Fort William.
Tel: (01397) 701 806.
www.limetreefortwilliam.co.uk

EATING OUT

Lime Tree Restaurant ★★

Possibly the best restaurant in Fort William, with an inventive menu.

Cameron Square,
Achintore Road,
Fort William.
Tel: (01397) 701 806.
www.limetreefortwilliam.co.uk

Crannog at the Waterfront ★★★

Superb location, perched above the waters of Fort William Harbour at the end of the pier, with equally great seafood.

Tel: (01397) 705 589.
www.oceanandoak.co.uk

SPORT AND LEISURE

Ice Factor

This amazing centre is regarded as one of the UK's finest activity centres. Facilities include climbing walls for all skill levels (from ten years and upwards) and the world's largest ice-climbing wall.

Kinlochleven, B863, 32km (20 miles) south of Fort William.
Tel: (01855) 831 100.
www.ice-factor.co.uk

Jacobite Steam Train

Spectacular 65km (40-mile) rail journey with views of Ben Nevis, the Caledonian Canal, the famous Glenfinnan Viaduct, Loch Shiel and Arisaig before arriving at Mallaig.

Fort William Station.
Tel: (01524) 737 751. www.westcoastrailways.co.uk.
Departures: May–Oct Mon–Fri 10.20am; return 4pm.

Lochaber Leisure Centre

Indoor pool, sauna, gym, squash courts and climbing wall are among the facilities here.

Belford Road, Fort William.
Tel: (01397) 704 359.
www.highland.gov.uk

Off Beat Bikes

Cycles to rent to suit all tastes and needs, from extreme trail bikes to tandems, child bikes, tagalongs and trailers.

117 High Street,
Fort William.
Tel: (01397) 704 008.
www.offbeatbikes.co.uk

Seal Island Cruises

Look out for seals, puffins and other seabirds – and perhaps even dolphins – on this 90-minute cruise from

Fort William to the nearby island seal colony. *Town Pier, Fort William. Tel: (01397) 700 714. www.crannog.net*

Inveraray
ACCOMMODATION
The Creggans Inn ★★
It's worth making a special detour to stay at this historic inn on the south shore of Loch Fyne, where the food is superb, the rooms and public areas cosy, and the staff very welcoming. Outstanding value for money, with a million-dollar view thrown in for free. *Strachur. Tel: (01369) 860 279. www.creggans-inn.co.uk*

Argyll Hotel ★★★
Built in the 18th century as the 'Great Inn' for visiting bigwigs, this historic hotel is comfortable and full of atmosphere. *Front Street, Inveraray. Tel: (01499) 302 466. www.the-argyll-hotel.co.uk*

Taychreggan Hotel ★★★
Cosy, country-house-style retreat overlooking Loch Awe, with its own fishing on the loch, activities such as falconry and clay shooting, and an excellent restaurant. *Kilchrenan, by Taynuilt. Tel: (01866) 833 211. www.taychregganhotel.co.uk*

EATING OUT
George Hotel Restaurant ★★
This gastro pub (which also has rooms) is the best place to eat in Inveraray town centre, with a seafood- and game-influenced menu and a capacious bar-restaurant with an open fireplace. *Main Street, Inveraray. Tel: (01499) 302 111. www.thegeorgehotel.co.uk*

Loch Fyne Seafood and Smokery ★★
Legendary seafood restaurant that has spawned a chain of franchise operations in England. Superb oysters, kippers and other fruits of the sea. Reservation recommended. *A83, 20km (12½ miles) north of Inveraray. Tel: (01499) 600 264.*

SPORT AND LEISURE
Inveraray Golf Club
This modest nine-hole golf course has grand views over Loch Fyne. *North Cromalt, Inveraray. Tel: (01499) 302 116.*

Loch Lomond
ACCOMMODATION
Rowardennan Youth Hostel ★
Unbeatable location right beside Loch Lomond and overlooked by Ben Lomond, within the national park. *Rowardennan, Loch Lomond. Tel: (01360) 870 259. www.syha.org.uk. Closed: Oct–Mar.*

De Vere Cameron House Hotel ★★★
Somewhat brash country-club-style hotel with indoor pool and leisure club, watersports, nine-hole golf course and its own lake cruiser. *Cameron House, Loch Lomond. Tel: (01389) 755 565. www.cameronhouse.co.uk*

The Lodge on Loch Lomond ★★★
Very stylish lochside hotel in this pretty village, with luxurious boutique-style rooms and an award-winning restaurant. The guest list has included two former US

presidents, apparently.
Luss, Loch Lomond.
Tel: (01436) 860 201.
www.loch-lomond.co.uk

EATING OUT
**Coach House Coffee
Shop ★**
Soup, sandwiches, teas
and cakes served on hand-
painted tartan crockery by
kilt-wearing waiters.
Luss, Loch Lomond.
Tel: (01436) 860 341.

ENTERTAINMENT
**Loch Lomond Sea Life
Aquarium**
Sharks, rays and colourful
coral reef creatures are on
display at this excellent all-
weather visitor attraction,
as well as water creatures
from the streams and
lochs of the Highlands
and the shores of the
North Sea and the Atlantic
Ocean. An excellent family
option for a rainy day.
*Lomond Shores, 1km
(²/₃ mile) north of
Balloch village centre.*
Tel: (0871) 423 2110.
www.sealifeeurope.com
Sweeney's Cruises
Sweeney's operates a fleet
of five cruise boats on
the loch.
The Pier, Balloch,

Loch Lomond.
Tel: (01389) 752 376.
www.sweeney.uk.com

SPORT AND LEISURE
**Can You Experience
Loch Lomond**
Canoeing, watersports,
walking and mountain
cycling, on and around
Loch Lomond.
*11 Haldane Terrace,
Balloch.*
Tel: (01389) 756 251.
www.canyouexperience.com

Oban
ACCOMMODATION
Barriemore Hotel ★★
Friendly and affordable
family-run guesthouse
with views of the bay.
Corran Esplanade, Oban.
*Tel: (01631) 566 356. www.
barriemore-hotel.co.uk*
Glenburnie Hotel ★★
This is a very pleasant
guesthouse with fine
views of the bay, on
Oban's sweeping
waterfront.
Corran Esplanade, Oban.
Tel: (01631) 562 089.
www.glenburnie.co.uk
Caledonian Hotel ★★★
Posh seafront hotel in the
centre of Oban with
recently refurbished
facilities, café, restaurant

and full hotel service.
Station Square, Oban.
Tel: (0844) 855 9136.
www.obancaledonian.com

EATING OUT
Ee-Usk ★★
Waterside bistro
restaurant with a great
fish menu (try the wild-
caught halibut) and an
adequate but not
extensive choice of wines.
North Pier, Oban.
Tel: (01631) 565 666.
www.eeusk.com
The Waterfront ★★
Excellent seafood that
could not be fresher, next
to the harbour and the
railway station.
Tel: (01631) 563 110.
www.waterfrontoban.co.uk
Coast ★★★
Fine modern Scottish
cooking emphasising
local, seasonal ingredients
– lamb, beef, poultry and
game in season.
104 George Street, Oban.
Tel: (01631) 569 900.
www.coastoban.co.uk

ENTERTAINMENT
**Skipinnish
Ceilidh House**
One of Scotland's top
traditional music venues,
with live bands, Highland

dancing, fiddle music and more, in a contemporary setting in the middle of Oban.
34–38 George Street, Oban. Tel: (01631) 569 599. www.skipinnish.com

Seafari Adventures
Marine ecotours offer the opportunity to see porpoises, whales, seals, otters and eagles.
Ellenabeich, Easdale, near Oban. Tel: (01852) 300 003. www.seafari.co.uk

INVERNESS AND AROUND
Beauly
ACCOMMODATION
Lovat Arms ★★
This family-owned inn has cosy bedrooms and serves good pub grub.
Main Street, Beauly. Tel: (01463) 782 313. www.lovatarms.com

EATING OUT
Beauly Tandoori ★★
Authentic South Asian dishes are much loved in Scotland and this restaurant in the centre of Beauly serves some of the best curries, biryanis and masala.

Beauly High Street. Tel: (01463) 782 221.

Inverness
ACCOMMODATION
Inverness Youth Hostel ★
This comfortable, modern youth hostel is just a few minutes' walk from the city centre and has private en-suite bedrooms and family rooms as well as bunk-bedded dormitories. It also has its own restaurant.
Victoria Drive, Inverness. Tel: (01463) 231 771. www.syha.org

Best Western Inverness Palace Hotel & Spa ★★★
Comfortable chain hotel with an excellent leisure club (with pool), free car parking and free Wi-Fi access and choice of brasserie and à la carte restaurants.
8 Ness Walk, Inverness. Tel: (01463) 223 243. www.bw-invernesspalace. co.uk

Culloden House ★★★★
Very grand country-house hotel in a Georgian manor house with de-luxe facilities (including a new pool), luxury suites and huge bedrooms.

Culloden village off the A9, 5km (3 miles) east of Inverness. Tel: (01463) 790 461. www.cullodenhouse.co.uk

Glenmoriston Townhouse Hotel ★★★★
Very chic and proportionately costly hotel beside the River Ness, which sets the benchmark for luxury accommodation in the city centre. Brasserie restaurant, à la carte restaurant and piano bar are among the trimmings. Swimming pool added in 2008.
20 Nessbank, Inverness. Tel: (01463) 223 777. www.glenmoristontown house.com

Rocpool Reserve ★★★★
Inverness's most stylish 'boutique hotel', with 11 designer rooms (2 of which have outdoor decks with hot tubs) and a very trendy bar and restaurant.
14 Culduthel Road, Inverness. Tel: (01463) 240 089. www.rocpool.com

EATING OUT
Castle Restaurant ★
This old-style town-centre café is the best

place in Inverness for a true Scottish fry-up – black pudding, bacon, sausages, fried eggs, haggis, fried bread and baked beans – or a meat-heavy lunch of chops, steak or a pie.

17 Castle Street, Inverness. Tel: (01463) 230 925.

Café 1 ★★

Excellent, modern brasserie-style restaurant that puts the emphasis on locally sourced, often organic produce.

10 Castle Street, Inverness. Tel: (01463) 226 200. www.cafe1.net

The Mustard Seed ★★

With great views of the river and a tasty modern menu that blends Highland produce with international style, The Mustard Seed is a long-established local favourite.

16 Fraser Street, Inverness. Tel: (01463) 226 200. www.themustardseed restaurant.co.uk

River Café ★★

This café-restaurant serves light snacks such as quiches and fishcakes, daily specials, and a richer evening menu of Highland classics such as scallops, salmon and Hebridean lamb.

10 Bank Street, Inverness. Tel: (01463) 714 884. www. invernessrestaurant.com

Abstract ★★★★

This sophisticated, French-influenced restaurant sets the standards for the best food in Inverness.

Glenmoriston Townhouse Hotel, 20 Nessbank, Inverness. Tel: (01463) 223 777. www.glenmoriston townhouse.com

ENTERTAINMENT

Bakoo

This independent club is regarded by hip young locals as the place to go for late nights out.

39 High Street, Inverness. Tel: (01463) 235 506.

G's Nightclub

G's has been Inverness's mainstream nightlife favourite for more than 20 years, and at weekends stays up later than anywhere else in town, with a licence until 3am.

9–21 Castle Street, Inverness. Tel: (01463) 233 322.

Hootananny

While its rivals (*see above*) feature DJs and club anthems for the local youth market, Hootananny has a more Celtic ambience, with the Ceilidh Bar hosting guest bands, stand-up comedy in the Bothy Bar, and more.

67 Church Street, Inverness. Tel: (01463) 233 651. www.hootananny.co.uk

SPORT AND LEISURE

Boots N Paddles

This outdoor adventure outfit arranges hillwalking, canoeing, abseiling, archery, gorge walking, rock climbing and mountain biking, with full equipment provided and pick-up from the address of your choice.

14 Cabrich, Kirkhill, Inverness. Tel: (0845) 612 5567. www. boots-n-paddles.co.uk

Cruise Loch Ness

This 60-passenger cruiser operates between Fort Augustus and Inverness and has an on-board café-bar.

Caledonian Canal, Fort Augustus. Tel: (01320) 366 277. www.cruiselochness.com

Inverness Aquadome

This huge leisure centre has pools, a gym, climbing walls, a running track, health suite and spa.

The Bught, Inverness.
Tel: (01463) 667 500.
www.invernessleisure.com

Jacobite Cruises

Frequent cruises on Loch Ness from just outside Inverness, with excellent views of Urquhart Castle and the loch and its surrounding scenery.

Tomnahurich Bridge,
Glenurquhart Road,
Inverness.
Tel: (01463) 233 999.
www.jacobite.co.uk

NORTHWEST HIGHLANDS

Ardnamurchan

ACCOMMODATION

Feorag House ★★★

Luxury self-catering cottages beside Loch Sunart, set in 5.2 hectares (13 acres) of grounds in which visitors may see red deer, otters and golden eagles.

Glenborrodale, Acharacle,
Kilchoan.
Tel: (01972) 500 248.
www.feorag.co.uk

Kilchoan House Hotel ★★★

Built in the late 19th century, this former shooting lodge has seven comfortable en-suite bedrooms, a cosy bar and splendid views over the Sound of Mull.

Kilchoan.
Tel: (01972) 510 200.
www.
kilchoanhousehotel.co.uk

EATING OUT

The White House ★★★

This excellent restaurant serves the best local organic produce from the west coast and the islands (including some superb seafood).

Lochaline,
Ardnamurchan.
Tel: (01967) 421 777.
www.thewhitehouse
restaurant.co.uk

ENTERTAINMENT

Clanranald Hotel

More a pub than a hotel (although it also has five cosy bedrooms), the Clanranald is owned by Highland squeezebox wizard Fergie MacDonald and at weekends is a magnet for local folk musicians.

Mingary, Acharacle,
Ardnamurchan.
Tel: (01967) 431 202.
www.clanranaldhotel.co.uk

SPORT AND LEISURE

Statesman Cruises

Daily boat cruises to Eas a Chual Aluinn, the highest waterfall in the UK, visiting seal colonies on the way.

Old Ferry Pier, Kylesku.
Tel: (01971) 502 345.

Assynt

ACCOMMODATION

Inchnadamph Lodge ★

This former shooting and angling lodge in the wilds of Assynt has bunks in the dormitory and some twin-bedded bedrooms, a shared kitchen and a canteen serving breakfast.

Inchnadamph, A837,
24km (15 miles) north of
Ullapool.
Tel: (01571) 822 218.
www.inch-lodge.co.uk

Inchnadamph Hotel ★★★

This hotel – a 200-year-old coaching inn – is the only option in the area for those looking for old-fashioned hotel service at a sensible price.

Inchnadamph,
A837, 24km (15 miles)

north of Ullapool.
Tel: (01571) 822 202. www.
inchnadamphhotel.co.uk

EATING OUT
**Inchnadamph Hotel
Restaurant ★★**
Traditional home-cooked
Scottish food, with an
emphasis on local
seafood, game such as
venison in season, pies
and puddings.
Inchnadamph, A837,
24km (15 miles) north
of Ullapool.
Tel: (01571) 822 202. www.
inchnadamphhotel.co.uk
Iolaire Restaurant ★★
This is the best restaurant
for miles around, located
in Lochinver's best hotel
and serving an excellent
menu which emphasises
fresh-caught seafood,
game, and local lamb
and beef.
Inver Lodge Hotel, Iolaire
Road, Lochinver.
Tel: (01571) 844 496.
www.inverlodge.com

SPORT AND LEISURE
Assynt Angling Group
This local anglers'
association welcomes
visiting fisherfolk and
has the low-down on
more than 150 trout and

salmon fishing in the
Assynt area. See their
website for details of
where to pick up local
fishing permits.
Lochinver, Assynt. No tel.
www.assyntangling.co.uk

Durness
ACCOMMODATION
Mackays ★★★
This cosy, stylish
restaurant with rooms in
the centre of Durness is
worth booking well in
advance, as it has just
seven attractively
furnished rooms.
Main Street, Durness.
Tel: (01971) 511 202.
www.visitmackays.com

EATING OUT
Balnakeil Bistro ★
Run-of-the-mill bistro
which is good for a
family lunch, serving
home-made soup, salads,
sandwiches, scones and
high teas.
Balnakeil Craft Village,
Durness.
Tel: (01971) 511 335.
Peatstacks ★★★
Durness's only
outstanding place to stay
is also the outstanding
place to eat in town.
Traditional Highland

produce includes Loch
Eriboll crab, lobster,
scallops and Sutherland
lamb.
Main Street, Durness.
Tel: (01971) 511 202.
www.visitmackays.com

SPORT AND LEISURE
Durness Golf Club
This wild and windswept
course by the sea is the
northernmost golf course
on the British mainland.
Balnakeil Bay, Durness.
Tel: (01971) 511 364.
www.durnessgolfclub.org

Gairloch
ACCOMMODATION
The Old Inn ★★
Simple rooms, not all of
which have en-suite
facilities, above a busy,
popular pub.
Old Bridge, Gairloch.
Tel: (0800) 542 5444.
www.theoldinn.net

EATING OUT
Mountain Restaurant ★★
This self-service café-
restaurant is almost like
vegetarian heaven; for
non-meat-eaters it is one
of the best options in the
whole of the Highlands.
Strath Square, Gairloch.
Tel: (01445) 712 316.

ENTERTAINMENT

The Old Inn

Live traditional music in this old-style pub on Tuesdays and Fridays and at weekends in summer.
Old Bridge, Gairloch.
Tel: (01445) 712 006.

Kyle of Lochalsh & Plockton

ACCOMMODATION

Plockton Hotel ★★

Hotel and cottage rooms in one of this area's prettiest villages, with excellent pub grub in the bar downstairs.
Shore Street, Plockton.
Tel: (01599) 544 274.
www.plocktonhotel.co.uk

EATING OUT

Plockton Shores ★

This affordable café-bistro by the sea in one of the region's prettiest villages serves breakfast, lunch and dinner as well as all-day snacks and sandwiches, all home cooked.
Shore Street, Plockton.
Tel: (01599) 544 263.

The Seafood Restaurant ★★★

Right on the platform at Kyle of Lochalsh's far-from-busy station, this is just the place to eat lunch or dinner while you wait for your train, bus or ferry.
Station Road,
Kyle of Lochalsh.
Tel: (01599) 534 813.
www.the-seafood-restaurant.co.uk

SPORT AND LEISURE

Leisure Marine

Seal-spotting trips on Loch Carron and the Inner Sound aboard the 50-passenger MV *Argus*. Leisure Marine also offers sea-angling trips and rents rowing boats, pedalos and canoes.

Mountain Beach

Bike hire, servicing, daily guided rides and longer cycling holidays on the mainland and islands.
5 Francis Street,
Dornie, Kyle of Lochalsh.
Tel: (01599) 555 739.
www.mountain-beach.co.uk

Ullapool

ACCOMMODATION

Ullapool Youth Hostel ★

Overlooking Loch Broom, this hostel has dorm bunks, en-suite rooms and family rooms. *Shore Street, Ullapool.*
Tel: (01854) 612 254.
www.syha.org.uk

Riverside Guest House ★★

Comfortable guesthouse with a mix of single, twin and double rooms and two family rooms, all with en-suite facilities.
Quay Street, Ullapool.
Tel: (01854) 612 239.
www.riversideullapool.com

Tanglewood House ★★★

This superbly stylish guesthouse sleeps up to six in three bedrooms in a beautiful modern house by the loch, and the food is cordon bleu.
Loch Broom, on the A835 just south of town,
Ulllapool.
Tel: (01854) 612 059.
www.tanglewoodhouse.co.uk

EATING OUT

The Tea Store ★

Old-fashioned café serving continental and fried breakfasts, lunch and teas with excellent home-baked scones and cakes, and a good choice of vegetarian dishes.
27 Argyle Street, Ullapool.
Tel: (01854) 612 995.
www.theteastore.co.uk

The Ceilidh Place ★★
The Ceilidh Place has a café-bar serving snacks and a restaurant with a very good seafood menu.
14 West Argyle Street, Ullapool.
Tel: (01854) 612 103.
www.ceilidhplace.com

ENTERTAINMENT
The Ceilidh Place
This funky, eclectic outfit offers live music, theatre and other events all year round and also has 11 bedrooms, bunk rooms, café-bar and bookshop.
14 West Argyle Street, Ullapool.
Tel: (01854) 612 103.
www.ceilidhplace.com

SPORT AND LEISURE
Loch Broom Leisure Centre
All-weather local leisure centre with 25m (82ft) indoor pool, climbing wall and sauna.
Quay Street, Ullapool.
Tel: (01854) 612 884. www. lochbroomleisure.co.uk
Ullapool Golf Course
This is an adequate if not wildly exciting nine-hole course. Club and trolley hire are available.

Morefield, North Road, Ullapool.
Tel: (01854) 613 323. www. ullapoolgolfclub.co.uk
West Highland Hawking
At this unusual attraction, visitors can spend time learning the basics of falconry with Harris hawks.
Hillhaven, Kinlochewe, Achnasheen.
Tel: (01445) 760 204.
www.westhighlandhawking. com

NORTHEAST HIGHLANDS
The Black Isle
SPORT AND LEISURE
North Kessock Dolphin and Seal Centre
Watch rare red kites on their nests using closed-circuit TV, or go on a seal- and dolphin-spotting cruise.
North Kessock.
Tel: (01463) 731 866.
www.wdcs.org

Dornoch
ACCOMMODATION
2 Quail ★★
This acclaimed restaurant in the centre of Dornoch also has three elegant and comfortable rooms, which are much in

demand, so booking well in advance is recommended.
Castle Street, Dornoch.
Tel: (01862) 811 811.
www.2Quail.com
Dornoch Castle Hotel ★★★
Comfortable and atmospheric hotel in a rather grand historic building in the middle of this attractive small town. The hotel has a good restaurant.
Castle Street, Dornoch.
Tel: (01862) 810 216. www. dornochcastlehotel.com

EATING OUT
Luigi's Café ★
Café and ice-cream parlour, popular with locals, serving light lunches, snacks, teas, cakes and ices.
1 Castle Street, Dornoch.
Tel: (01862) 810 893.
www.luigidornoch.com

SPORT AND LEISURE
Royal Dornoch Golf Club
Formed in 1877, the Royal Dornoch is a mature links course that is regularly rated as one of the world's 15 best courses. Five new holes

have recently been added, and facilities include a modern clubhouse, pro shop, and equipment rental.
Golf Road, Dornoch.
Tel: (01862) 810 219.
www.royaldornoch.com

Helmsdale
ACCOMMODATION
Helmsdale Youth Hostel ★
This small hostel in Helmsdale has just 24 beds and bunks, some of them in private rooms.
Stafford Street, Helmsdale.
Tel: (0870) 155 3255.
www.syha.org.uk
Bridge Hotel ★★
Antlers and stuffed deer heads abound in this shooting-lodge-style hotel with 19 well-designed and attractive modern rooms.
Dunrobin Street, Helmsdale.
Tel: (01431) 821 100.
www.bridgehotel.net

EATING OUT
La Mirage ★★★
Despite its name and film-star glamorous décor, this friendly little restaurant has an unpretentious menu that includes the best fish and chips for miles around. Also has two self-catering rooms for rent.
Dunrobin Street, Helmsdale.
Tel: (01431) 821 615.
www.lamirage.org

SPORT AND LEISURE
Panning for gold
Gold dust and small nuggets can still be found in the Bal an Or burn (stream) near Helmsdale and would-be prospectors can rent gold-panning equipment from Strath Ullie Crafts in the village centre.
The Harbour, Shore Street, Helmsdale.
Tel: (01431) 821 402.
www.helmsdale.org

Strathpeffer
ACCOMMODATION
Ben Wyvis Hotel ★★★
Comfortably grand hotel, located in its own manicured grounds in the middle of Strathpeffer village.
Town centre, Strathpeffer.
Tel: (0870) 950 6264.
www.crerarhotels.com
Coul House Hotel ★★★
This hotel offers country-house style at a reasonable price and is conveniently located for touring travellers. It has a good restaurant and is set in attractive grounds.
Contin, at the A834/ A835 junction, 7km (4 miles) south of Strathpeffer.
Tel: (01997) 421 487.
www.coulhousehotel.com

EATING OUT
Jacobite Restaurant ★★★
The excellent restaurant of the Ben Wyvis Hotel serves organic local produce, beef, fish and game.
Ben Wyvis Hotel, town centre, Strathpeffer.
Tel: (0870) 950 6264.
www.crerarhotels.com

ENTERTAINMENT
Coul House Hotel
The hotel has live traditional music on Friday and Saturday evenings in summer.
See Accommodation, above.

SPORT AND LEISURE
Strathpeffer Golf Club
Legendary golf course that opened in 1888, standing in beautiful surroundings on the

outskirts of Strathpeffer.
*Golf Course Road,
Strathpeffer.
Tel: (01997) 421 219.
www.strathpeffergolf.co.uk*

Thurso
ACCOMMODATION
Sandra's Hostel ★
Unassuming modern
hostel in town centre,
with its own takeaway
snack bar, free Internet
access and continental
breakfast included.
*24 Princes Street, Thurso.
Tel: (0845) 293 7373.
www.syha.org.uk*
Forss House Hotel ★★★
Luxurious country-house
hotel in its own wooded
grounds overlooking the
sea. Acclaimed restaurant.
*Forss, A836, 8km
(5 miles) west of Thurso.
Tel: (01847) 861 201.
www.forsshousehotel.
co.uk*

EATING OUT
The Captain's Galley ★★
This excellent seafood
restaurant uses all local
ingredients and the fish
is superbly fresh.
*The Harbour,
Scrabster, Thurso.
Tel: (01847) 894 999.
www.captainsgalley.co.uk*

ENTERTAINMENT
All Star Factory
Thurso's local cinema
screens run-of-the mill
mainstream films
soon after their UK
premiere.
*Ormlie Road, Thurso.
Tel: (01847) 890 890.*

SPORT AND LEISURE
**Caithness Sea Angling
Association**
For details of sea-fishing
trips from Thurso and
Scrabster, as well as
whale- and dolphin-
spotting day cruises,
contact the association.
*Tel: (01847) 893 179.
www.sport.caithness.org*

Wick & John O'Groats
ACCOMMODATION
**John O'Groats
Youth Hostel ★**
This hostel has bunk
beds and private rooms,
and magnificent sea
views from its windows.
*Canisbay, John O'Groats.
Tel: (01955) 611 761.
www.syha.org.uk*
Quayside B&B ★★
Friendly, no-nonsense
bed-and-breakfast
guesthouse. Few frills,
but central and cosy.
Harbour Quay, Wick.

*Tel: (01955) 603 229.
www.quaysidewick.fsnet.
co.uk*
Mackay's Hotel ★★★
This dignified old hotel,
opened in 1833, is the
most luxurious place to
stay in Wick.
*1 Ebenezer Place, Wick.
Tel: (01955) 602 323.
www.mackayshotel.co.uk*

EATING OUT
No 1 Bistro ★★★
The menu at the bistro
restaurant of Wick's best
hotel emphasises fresh
fish and local produce.
*Mackay's Hotel,
1 Ebenezer Place, Wick.
Tel: (01955) 602 323.
www.mackayshotel.co.uk*

SPORT AND LEISURE
**John O'Groats Ferries
Wildlife Cruises**
John O'Groats Ferries
operates daily wildlife
cruises to see puffins,
gannets and other
seabirds, dolphins and
seals.
*John O'Groats Harbour.
Tel: (01955) 611 353.
www.jogferry.co.uk*

Index

Acknowledgements

Thomas Cook Publishing wishes to thank SCOTTISH VIEWPOINT, to whom the copyright belongs, for the photographs in this book, except for the following images:

DREAMSTIME.COM 1 (R M HAYMAN), 22 (AVW1806), 62 (MARTIN SEVCIK), 118 (JOHN CARTER)

All SCOTTISH VIEWPOINT images were taken by PAUL TOMKINS/VISITSCOTLAND, except: 45, 78 (D BARNES); 19, 124 (D HABRON); 40 (SCOTTISH VIEWPOINT); 14, 44, 54, 56, 57, 58, 60, 73, 84, 85, 93, 97, 119, 131, 140, 141, 149 (VISITSCOTLAND).

For CAMBRIDGE PUBLISHING MANAGEMENT LIMITED:
Project editor: Kate Taylor
Typesetter: Paul Quer
Proofreaders: Kelly V
Indexer: Karolin Thor

D YOUR THO   TS TO
BO   @THOMA   )K.COM

We're co   providing the very be   late information in
our trave   constantly strive to   n as useful as they
can be. Y   p us to i   ve futur   by letting us have
your fee   ou've made a wonderf   ry on your travels
that we   dy feature, if you'd lik   n us about recent
changes   that we include   imply want to let us
know yo   about this guidebo   w we can make it even
better –   to hear from you.

Send   tter and records   s today and then look
out for   this title.

Ema   weller guides
Series E   Thomas   227, Coningsby Road,
Peterborough PE3 8SB, UK.

Please don't forget to let us know which title your feedback refers to!